MALIBU FARM
SUNRISE TO SUNSET

MALIBU FARM SUNRISE to SUNSET

SIMPLE RECIPES ALL DAY

HELENE HENDERSON

PHOTOGRAPHS BY ERIN KUNKEL

CLARKSON POTTER/PUBLISHERS
NEW YORK

Also by Helene Henderson

MALIBU FARM COOKBOOK

CONTENTS

10 FROM SUNRISE TO SUNSET

24 SUNRISE BREAKFAST

63 MIDDAY LUNCH

133 AFTERNOON FIKA

170 SUNSET DINNER

256 SKÅL! AFTER-DINNER DRINKS AND SNACKS

294 COOKING RULES

296 GRATITUDE + APPRECIATION + ACKNOWLEDGMENTS + RECOGNITION

298 INDEX

Cafe

FROM SUNRISE TO SUNSET

I had never heard of Malibu, surfers, or female chefs when I was growing up, and I had never aspired to be a chef or restaurateur, but here I am on the Malibu Pier, running two restaurants overlooking a world-famous surf break. And somehow I also ended up with waterfront Malibu Farm restaurants in Newport Beach, Lanai, Miami, New York, Los Cabos, and Zushi Marina in Kanagawa, Japan.

How did I get here? I really don't know. Maybe through the back door, through the alley, through some passageway I didn't know existed or even dreamed about. Sometimes you can't enter through the front door; sometimes there is no path. You have to clear your own way and create your own journey, and mine started in the very north of Sweden.

As a teenager I headed off alone to New York City, without a plan or a mission. My pockets were empty, my English was poor, I knew nobody, but I had a heart full of dreams and hope. After one year in the Big Apple with random jobs in retail and a few stints modeling, I followed a new friend and headed west. In Los Angeles, I first worked in graphic design, then as a server for a catering company, and later as a chef for event planners Along Came Mary, LA Celebrations, and Somerset Catering.

I learned the trade and eventually started my own catering company, Lavender Farms, which I ran out of my home kitchen in Hollywood. I arrived at events in an old beat-up Toyota Land Cruiser. It was a one-woman (non-permitted) operation, but I still was able to cater large events for celebrities, movie studios, and corporations. Although my husband, John, suggested it many times, I never believed in myself enough to rent a commercial kitchen and invest in a catering van. Instead of going legit with my catering company, I became a private chef.

It was John's dream to move to Malibu, and we saved like crazy to make that dream a reality in 2008. I am a Malibu local now, but unlike my husband, who is an avid surfer, I never go to the beach. I don't even own a swimsuit. I can't swim or surf, and even in the shallowest bodies of water I sink like a rock. I have been known to get seasick on the pier, and I might be allergic to sand, if that is a thing. Forests, farms, and gardens are where I belong. Or so I thought.

Malibu Farm began as a hobby. I was a private chef in the evenings, and I taught cooking classes from my home during the day. The classes evolved into farm dinners in my backyard in the Point Dume neighborhood of Malibu. I started the Malibu Farm cooking blog to post recipes, and my classes and events soon grew in size and in frequency. My little residential street was often filled with the cars of guests attending classes and dinners at my underground (and illegal) backyard restaurant. Eventually the City of Malibu shut me down, as was only right; commercial activity requires a permit, and only four events are allowed per year, per home, and I was often doing three events per weekend. So although there was a demand for the dinners I was offering, I had nowhere to host them. Sometimes I was able to partner with a local farm or ranch, but my options were limited. I hoped for a more permanent commercial location in a garden or farm setting.

John maintains that I cried when he first proposed to me that I do a Malibu Farm pop-up cafe in the shuttered Ruby's Diner at the end of the Malibu Pier. That's a huge overstatement—but I was dreaming of a farm location, not a 1980s diner with red vinyl seats and white plastic tables. The view, although spectacular, was not of a farm. There was no garden. There was no vineyard. There were no fruit trees. The pier at the time was a deserted and neglected historical gem, and the only people there were fishers, vagrants, and the occasional derelict. Now that the pier is bustling with life, it seems crazy that it was vacant for years. Two empty waterfront restaurant spaces were just waiting for someone to come along to love them and bring them back to life.

This pop-up cafe would sail me away from the farm location of my dreams and out onto a funky pier. But it was the only option in front of me, so my designer friend Vanessa Alexander and I ripped out the red vinyl banquettes and white plastic tables. In the kitchen I replaced the deep fryers with convection ovens. I tossed out the massive lines of soda dispensers and bought an undercounter fridge to hold freshly squeezed juices. We built some farm tables, and slowly but surely it started to look a little bit like me, except for the fact that I was out to sea.

I spent about $40,000 to open the cafe, an inheritance from my mother—the amount she was awarded in a medical malpractice suit, the malpractice that ultimately took her life. She had always worried that I would end up broke and alone in America, with nobody left in Sweden to take care of me. Before she passed away, she made me promise that I would not forget Sweden, and that I would use her money to build a new business. And so I did. I opened a pop-up cafe. I didn't know if it would fail or succeed—I only knew that I had done as I promised. My mother passed away in the spring of 2012 and never knew that Malibu Farm became a real business.

I was fifty years old, I was opening a restaurant, and I did not have a clue. Although I had been employed in restaurants as a teenager in Sweden, in my adult life I had held jobs only in the catering and private chef world. Operating a restaurant was a completely new experience. My opening front-of-house crew was two Pepperdine students who had worked on the backyard dinners with me. In the kitchen, there was me and two cooks I hired from a nearby restaurant. I set the cafe up like it was a catering operation. We did not have a point-of-sale system. Instead, we had iPhones with Square Readers. The night before we opened, my husband swung by and said, "How will the kitchen know what the customers order?" Slight detail—we had not set up any ticket printers. When a customer orders food, a ticket is supposed to print in the kitchen alerting the cooks what to make. With no printers, we had to hand-write paper tickets. Very time-consuming. Yeah, there was a lot to learn.

I opened for breakfast and lunch simply because I still had my private chef job at night, and in my estimation and everyone else's expectations, the pop-up would fail. I just needed to survive the six-month term without going broke. My job making dinner for a family of four paid enough to cover the costs of my pier employees. I had to be at that job at 5 p.m., so the pier cafe was open from 9 a.m. to 3 p.m.

One of the very first customers to stroll into the cafe ended up coming in for breakfast daily. One day a cafe cashier said "mayor" wanted to meet me. I thought, the mayor of what or where? I went out to say hello and soon learned that this man's name was Meir, not a mayor. Meir Teper was an owner of the Nobu restaurants, and I still don't know how he found me and my little cafe. Destiny? Coincidence? The force of the Pacific swell? We started talking, and along the way he became a mentor to my underground brand and crucial to the growth of the business. Lanai, Miami, New York, and Los Cabos all came to fruition because I had met "The Mayor."

Life on the pier, where I am captain of my independent brand, has been blessed with spectacular views, but it has not been easy. We have sometimes been adrift without a compass or direction, we have been lost at sea, we have fought to stay afloat, but somehow we have sailed through rough patches, storms, hurricanes, and fires—and we are still here.

There was much more to learn than how to cook food for crowds, build a menu, and run a restaurant. Those were the expected things. I also found out that a single tossed cigarette can close your business down. I learned this the hard way, when our cafe deck caught fire after a fisher left a smoldering cigarette and our deck went up in flames. Every day to this day, I stop pier visitors from smoking. I have been called "Officer Henderson" more times than I can count. I also learned that trash from the end of the pier must travel in a small pushcart one mile to reach the dumpster at the end of the parking lot, and deliveries must travel from the parking lot down to the cafe. This requires a fleet of full-time custodians to push trash carts or deliveries up and down the pier, for the cafe and the restaurant, back and forth. I learned that when you operate on a pier and hundreds of beachgoers use your restrooms and trash containers daily, this creates a full-time job for several employees, long lines, frustrated customers, and a huge expense when you exceed the pier wastewater capacity.

There were battles between the fishers and the customers, and as Officer Henderson I often had to intervene. The Malibu Pier is, after all, a sportfishing pier and fishers are everywhere, but some customers who proudly tell you they eat wild-caught Alaska salmon will freak out when someone catches a fish in front of them. I guess it is not clear to them where their fish actually comes from, or they really just don't want to know. I also learned the most important lesson of them all, which is that restaurants are all about people, and finding and retaining good staff is the most challenging of all tasks. I lucked out with an amazing team, and most of them are still here on the pier with me today.

Cafe
MALIBU
FARM

In August 2014, Hurricane Marie brought the biggest swell in decades. It also brought us to our knees and almost brought down the pier. We ran for our lives that day—all right, an exaggeration, but not really, as the pier shook like crazy, waves crashed overhead, and thirty pier pylons came loose and washed ashore. The pier was temporarily red-tagged, but once again, the waves of life carried the little cafe forward. We were sometimes underwater, but we would resurface again and again.

That same year a second restaurant would open at the front of the pier in the larger, more glamorous location. They had a rock-star chef with a pedigree name, and a cool kitchen crew with tattoos and piercings. They had chef jackets with their names on them, while we didn't even have jackets. I was told that "real chefs" were taking over the pier, and I believed them. I prepared for the worst, thinking that the front restaurant would take all the pier business and my restaurant journey had reached its end.

They had a better location, eye-popping ocean views, a professional restaurant group, and a real chef. I still, and probably always will, consider myself a "cooler lady" from all my years of lugging around a cooler for catering and private chef work. I can't really wrap my head around the "chef" label. However, the new restaurant failed to connect with the local customers and closed after just nine months. The cool chefs packed their knives and left, and so we took over their larger front restaurant as well.

I was on the water and I was treading water, barely staying afloat, with two restaurants, almost 450 seats, no real restaurant experience, 200 employees, and ocean views as far as you could see. We did full service for the first time, and our service was "terrible, horrible, no good, very bad" to start. The cafe was counter service, which means you fetch your own ketchup and water, which is not the same as a full-service restaurant. With two Malibu Farm restaurants close together, we struggled to differentiate between them. At the larger restaurant we had a full bar for the first time and needed a cocktail program, so David Shoham, our general manager, created a menu of all-organic agave-based signature drinks. The cafe and the restaurant were the same yet different, and we swam against the current to stay current, to stay inclusive, and to cook for people, not for our egos.

Against all odds, we survived. Several visually sensational waterfront locations followed: Newport Beach, Lanai, Miami, New York, Los Cabos, and Kanagawa. We fought a lot of battles and had some failures and many successes.

Everyone wanted to change us, change me, improve me, by making me more upscale, but I didn't want to be more exclusive. I wanted to remain inclusive and casual. And every man wanted to tell me he knew better. Traveling a path as a woman outside the system isn't easy, but I didn't need to be changed or rescued. For the first time in my life, I realized, I was not lost. I had finally found myself. I knew exactly who I was and who I wanted to be. I don't want fine dining. I want home cooking and simple recipes, and I want everyone to eat their vegetables! I don't want to talk about folding napkins or have different fragile glasses for every beverage. I want grandparents and kids to feel comfortable here. I want restaurants that feel like a home, not like dining out. I want the service to feel friendly, not like being waited on by servants.

And just when you think you have things figured out, everything changes.

November 9, 2018, started like any other day in Malibu—warm and beautiful—and it ended in devastation for our community. Although Malibu is prone to fires, and perhaps they should be expected, the fury and roar of the Woolsey fire took everyone by surprise. When the weekend was over, six hundred homes had been lost, including one hundred in my immediate neighborhood. We were lucky—our house was spared—but the fire came close and much of our landscape burned. There were no firefighters in sight that weekend, but the Point Dume "*bomberos*"—teenagers, locals, young and old, including our son Casper, his friends, and our opening chef Dane—helped save many houses that weekend, including ours. I still can't believe that in the midst of the fire my daughter, Celia, who lives out of state and was the only one with a working phone, reached Big Heart Ranch, and they got every chicken, Arnold the pig, and the goats captured and corralled into a trailer and evacuated. The animals spent two weeks at the ranch before it was safe for them to return. They said Arnold was a good eater and even ate Brussels sprouts. I'm not sure what they were talking about; he is an extremely picky eater!

Once the danger was over and the fires extinguished, our city and its residents faced a new day. The fire was a reality check: the life we have today is not guaranteed tomorrow. The Malibu Pier restaurants were closed for a while, and the journey back to business as usual was long and difficult, but our Malibu Farm team members rose to the challenges of roadblocks and road closures and a massive cleanup of the restaurant (power was out for over one week and all the refrigerated and frozen foods had spoiled). It would take months before customers returned to our city, but each day we staffed up and prepped up and opened our doors and our hearts and hoped for visitors and locals to return and dine with us again. Labor costs alone would exceed income for weeks, and slow weeks would turn into slow months.

Then in January 2019 the heavens opened and rain came pouring down. The rain was bad for business and the financial losses continued. The roads were frequently closed due to the risk of mudslides, but luckily our city experienced no major rain damage. Many locals were still evacuated and tourists stayed away. But then after months of rain, more than we had received in 144 years, our burned hillsides turned to blossoming beauties, with green, yellow, and purple flowers everywhere and butterflies all around. It was breathtaking and reaffirming. Life would go on. Our scarred city became more beautiful than ever. Recovery was up and down, and it didn't happen overnight or as fast as we wanted, but slowly life returned to a new normal.

And one by one, everyone and everything returned—the guests, the locals, the wildlife, the calm ocean breeze—and with the breeze a good meal with family and friends. Life settled into what seemed like normal, or so we thought. The year 2020 was off to a great start and held promise for a drama-free year. Then out of nowhere the coronavirus spread across the globe, and it became clear that "normal" seasons, projections, plans, and expectations were a thing of the past. Malibu Farm Japan was scheduled to open on March 26, 2020, at the height of the outbreak, and those plans of course were put on hold. My restaurants, all restaurants, the entire country, faced a new threat—pandemic, isolation, quarantine—words we had never considered part of our everyday vocabulary. But they were fact and not movie fiction. And so once again I was reminded that we don't know what will happen or what to expect tomorrow. The only thing we can do is treasure every moment and every meal. We can start each day with a hope of tomorrow. The pop-up cafe opened first for breakfast, and morning is my favorite time of the day. That is how I began, and also how this book begins. With breakfast. A new day is when new opportunities begin. To start, you must have breakfast, the most important meal, because it launches the daily journey and helps you discover the possibilities of the new day.

When I wrote the first Malibu Farm cookbook, I had no idea what was up ahead, not a clue that my hobby was a little seed that could, and would, grow beyond anyone's imagination. The original cookbook was based on the cooking classes and the backyard dinners. It was written and photographed in the summer of 2012, one full year before the original pop-up cafe opportunity presented itself, and therefore none of the restaurant recipes were included. Now we are sharing them with you.

We invite you on a journey, from sunrise to sunset, from morning to night. Start your day with Surfers Rancheros (page 53) or Vegan Chocolate Banana Pancakes (page 39). Then pull up a beach chair and join us for lunch with Vegetable-Crust Pizzas (page 67) and Grilled Salmon Kale Niçoise Salad (page 73). Afternoon is *fika* time, also known as coffee, tea, and treats. It's a moment to refuel with the ultimate berry meringue (page 143) or Vegan Cashew Coconut Cherry Ice Cream (page 137). And as the day comes to an end and the sun sets, we fire up the barbecue so we can grill our steaks (page 224) and our kale (page 193). Then before the night is over we will pour a drink—to our health or for our health, it is cheers and *Skål*—our glasses filled with frozen rosé (page 261) or horchata (page 266), while we snack on tacos (page 284), caramel popcorn (page 290), and olive oil chocolate-dipped treats (page 289).

My hope with this book is that it will inspire you to cook more at home, to cook without recipes and with confidence. That the uncomplicated instructions and combinations will make your home-cooked meals sing a song of simplicity and authenticity, and that you will go on to create dishes on your own. I hope you will feel confident enough in the kitchen to use ingredients you love and skip those you don't, but also to be adventurous enough to try something new from Malibu.

SUNRISE BREA

KFAST

California is *the* "**GOOD MORNING**" state. Every time the **SUN** rises there is a possibility and an opportunity for trials and errors, successes and failures, to give and to receive, and to **NEVER GIVE UP.** We believe we can and will change the world, and as Malibu dreamers we hope to lead our nation into the future, to **EAT HEALTHIER,** to learn and grow, to travel and explore, to hike, surf, and run, to **FIND LOVE AND GIVE LOVE,** to nurture and be nurtured. We start each day with a **HEALTHY BREAKFAST,** and in the spirit of our state, healthy options also include **COMFORT FOODS,** vegan choices, and gluten-free selections.

I began my journey as a restaurant owner with breakfast service, and that is my **FAVORITE MEAL** of the day. All our locations are on the waterfront, and regardless of where we are, we begin our mornings with the sound of the **WAVES,** the sight of the **SEA,** and the warmth of the **SUN.**

From our breakfast table to yours, **GOOD MORNING**!

ACAI BREAKFAST BOWL

SERVES 1

1 cup frozen mixed berries

¼ banana

1 (3½-ounce) package acai puree (see Tip)

½ cup almond milk (or any milk or milk alternative of your choice)

OPTIONAL GARNISHES: granola (see Note) and sliced fresh fruit or berries

NOTE For a recipe to make your own granola, refer to my first book, *Malibu Farm Cookbook*, page 41.

TIP Instead of using individual packets of acai puree, you could purchase a pint-size package and use an ice cream scoop to measure it out.

Oh, the places you'll go, the people you'll know. Beyond your imagination lies a world of inspiration. Start your day in a spectacular way with this ultimate Malibu beach breakfast smoothie in a bowl.

Combine the berries, banana, acai puree, and milk in a blender and whirl for 30 seconds. Transfer the puree to a cute little dish, garnish as you wish, and begin your day.

EARTH MOTHER YOGURT BOWL

SERVES 2

1 papaya, pineapple, or other large, hard-shelled fruit

2 cups plain yogurt (whole milk or cashew; see Note)

1 tablespoon maple syrup or other sweetener of choice (optional)

A few vanilla seeds scraped from a vanilla bean (optional)

1 cup granola

1 cup assorted berries or sliced fruit, for garnish

NOTE My favorite vegan yogurt is Forager Cashewmilk; I use the vanilla one for ice cream and sweet recipes. For savory recipes like Lime Cucumber Yogurt Sauce (page 277), I use the unsweetened plain version. For a coconut granola recipe, see my first book, *Malibu Farm Cookbook*, page 41.

TIP Rather than buying flavored yogurt, which I usually find too sweet, I add fruit to plain whole-milk yogurt to sweeten it.

It takes mere minutes to upgrade your morning from simple to simply spectacular by serving breakfast in a bowl that Mother Nature created. There is nothing more inviting, or easier, than carving out a bowl from a papaya, pineapple, or other fruit and loading it up with the yogurt of your choice, topped with granola and garnished with berries and fruit.

Cut your papaya, pineapple, or other fruit in half and remove the seeds or core. Scoop out 3 tablespoons of the fruit flesh, mash it in a small bowl, and stir it into the plain yogurt.

I like my yogurt on the tart side, but if you like more sweetness, mix in a little maple syrup or other sweetener and a few vanilla seeds.

To serve, spoon the yogurt into the scooped-out fruit bowls, and top with the granola. Garnish with berries or other fruit as desired.

COCONUT BERRY FRENCH TOAST

SERVES 4

¾ cup white or brown sugar

6 large eggs

3 cups coconut milk, heavy cream, or half-and-half

1 teaspoon vanilla extract

5 slices brioche bread, cubed

1 pint blackberries or other berries of choice, or 1 cup sautéed sliced apples or pears

OPTIONAL GARNISH: Top with whipped cream and additional fruit

TIP Feeding a crowd? Bake this in one large skillet or baking dish, rather than as individual servings.

This baked French toast is an indulgent farm-chic dish, and so easy to make. You can prepare it the day before and then in the morning, just pop it in the oven for 25 minutes. Ready, set, serve. It is so delicious, you can also serve it as a dessert!

The best choice for these ramekins is four small cast-iron skillets.

Preheat the oven to 375°F.

Spoon 1 tablespoon of the sugar into each individual cast-iron skillet. Place each skillet on a burner and melt the sugar over medium heat until it becomes caramelized, about 2 minutes. Do not stir or touch the sugar while it melts, or else it might crystallize. Leave it alone and it will melt into brown caramel goodness. Remove the skillets from the heat so that the caramel does not burn. Set them aside and let cool.

In a large bowl, whisk together the eggs, coconut milk, ¼ cup of the remaining sugar, and the vanilla. Once they are well combined, stir in the brioche cubes and let them soak up the liquid.

Pour the brioche cubes over the hardened caramel in the skillets. Stir in the berries or other fruit. Sprinkle the remaining ¼ cup sugar lightly over the tops.

Bake in the oven for about 25 minutes, until the custard is just set and the top is browned.

If you like, top each serving with whipped cream and extra fruit.

I HEART YOU GLUTEN-FREE WAFFLES

SERVES 4

3 large eggs

3 cups whole milk

½ cup sour cream or crème fraîche

1½ tablespoons salted butter, melted

¼ cup white or brown sugar

½ teaspoon salt

½ teaspoon ground cardamom or cinnamon (optional)

2½ cups gluten-free flour (I recommend Bob's Red Mill gluten-free all-purpose baking flour)

Nonstick cooking spray

FOR SERVING: whipped cream, maple syrup, and gluten-free granola; a berry compote; or whipped cream with fresh berries

TIP For a rich topping, fold a few tablespoons of your favorite jam into 1 cup of whipped cream.

In Sweden, waffles are always heart-shaped and very, very thin. For many years I wanted these waffles for my restaurant. I searched and searched for the right waffle iron. They are easy to find for home use, but commercial heart-shaped Swedish-style restaurant waffle irons were hard to locate, until one day I finally found them. Where? Online from China, of course.

We set out to create a recipe that reminded me of my childhood but was also gluten-free. You can use any standard waffle iron here, but I recommend tracking down a Nordic-style heart-shaped one. We top our waffles several ways: with whipped cream, maple syrup, and gluten-free granola for a nice crunch, or with a berry compote, or with whipped cream with fresh berries. It's your choice!

Whisk together all the wet ingredients (eggs, milk, sour cream, and butter) in one medium bowl and all the dry ingredients (sugar, salt, cardamom, if using, and flour) in another. Slowly add the dry ingredients to the wet ingredients, stirring steadily until the wet and dry ingredients are combined. Let the batter sit at room temperature for about 30 minutes. (The batter can also be made a day in advance and kept in the fridge.)

Spray a preheated waffle iron with nonstick cooking spray, and spoon just enough batter into the iron to fill it. Close the waffle iron and cook until the waffle is brown and crisp on both sides, 3 to 5 minutes.

Serve the waffles with the toppings of your choice.

PUMPKIN PANCAKES + CRISPY OATS

SERVES 4

1 cup sour cream or crème fraîche

3 large eggs

1 cup canned pumpkin puree

1 teaspoon vanilla extract

1 cup cooked quinoa

1¼ cups gluten-free flour (I recommend Bob's Red Mill gluten-free all-purpose baking flour)

2 tablespoons brown or white sugar

1 teaspoon baking soda

1 teaspoon baking powder

¼ teaspoon salt

4 tablespoons salted butter

About 4 tablespoons olive oil

½ cup Coconut Crispy Oats (page 42)

½ cup Cubed Roasted Butternut Squash (page 54)

Maple syrup, for serving

NOTE The pancake batter can be made up to 2 days ahead and stored in the fridge.

VEGAN OPTION Want vegan pumpkin pancakes? Follow the recipe for Vegan Chocolate Banana Pancakes on page 39, substituting pumpkin puree for the banana, and garnish and finish per this recipe.

I love pancakes and I love pumpkins, and I know my favorite season is here when pumpkin pancakes are on the menu. We garnish them with crispy oats and cubes of roasted butternut squash. And can you also add bacon bits? Hmm, well, yes, you can.

In a medium bowl, whisk together the wet ingredients (sour cream, eggs, pumpkin puree, vanilla, and quinoa). In another medium bowl, combine the dry ingredients (flour, sugar, baking soda, baking powder, and salt). Slowly add the dry ingredients to the wet ingredients, stirring steadily until the wet and dry ingredients are well combined.

Preheat a large skillet over medium heat. Add 1 tablespoon of the butter and 1 tablespoon of the olive oil and heat until melted. Spoon ½ cup of the pancake batter per pancake into the skillet (the number of pancakes will depend on the size of your skillet). Cook until bubbles appear on the surface of the pancakes, about 2 minutes, and then flip them over and cook until the pancakes are cooked through, about 2 minutes. Transfer the pancakes to a large plate or platter and keep covered, or place in the oven on low temperature until ready to serve. Repeat, adding more oil and butter for each batch of pancakes.

To serve, top the pancakes with the Coconut Crispy Oats and cubed butternut squash, and drizzle with maple syrup.

FRERES
LERIE
CÔTE D'OR
NCE

VEGAN CHOCOLATE BANANA PANCAKES

SERVES 4

1 cup (8 ounces) silken (soft) tofu (see Tip on page 40)

1 cup chocolate oat milk (see Tip on page 40 if you can't find this at the store)

3 ripe bananas

3 tablespoons brown sugar

½ teaspoon vanilla extract

1¼ cups gluten-free flour (I recommend Bob's Red Mill gluten-free all-purpose baking flour)

½ teaspoon baking soda

1 teaspoon baking powder

¼ teaspoon salt

¾ cup cooked quinoa

Olive oil, vegetable oil, or vegan butter

Maple syrup, for serving

Confectioners' sugar, for serving

Coconut Crispy Oats, for serving (recipe follows)

NOTE The pancake batter can be made up to 2 days ahead and stored in the fridge.

Pancakes topped with whipped cream and berries will always hold a special place in my heart and in my world, but the world has changed. And we should and must aspire to change with it. Vegans are no longer few and far between. For our restaurant, this meant we needed a vegan pancake option. It took a few trials, but then it finally came together. These pancakes are vegan and gluten-free, but *shh,* don't tell. The eggs, dairy, and wheat will not be missed. They are now my favorite pancakes, so even old dogs (and mature cats like me) can learn new tricks. I am pretty sure these pancakes will become your family favorite.

Combine the tofu, chocolate oat milk, 1½ bananas, the brown sugar, and the vanilla in a blender and process until smooth.

In a large bowl combine the dry ingredients (flour, baking soda, baking powder, and salt). Pour the blended tofu-and-banana mixture into the dry ingredients and combine to form a smooth batter. Then stir in the quinoa.

Place a large skillet over medium heat. Add 2 tablespoons oil or vegan butter, and heat until melted. Spoon ½ cup of the pancake batter per pancake into the skillet (the number of pancakes will depend on the size of your skillet). Cook until bubbles appear on the surface of the pancakes, about 2 minutes. Then flip them over and cook on the other side until cooked through, about 2 more minutes. Transfer the

(RECIPE CONTINUES)

pancakes to a large plate or platter and keep covered, or place in the oven on low temperature until ready to serve. Repeat, adding more oil or vegan butter for each batch of pancakes.

Once all the batter is used up, slice the remaining 1½ bananas. Add a little oil to the same skillet and sauté the banana slices over medium heat for 1 to 2 minutes, until browned on all sides.

Serve the pancakes garnished with the sautéed bananas, a drizzle of maple syrup, and a sprinkling of confectioners' sugar. For crunch, add some Coconut Crispy Oats.

TIPS Make vegan sour cream with the remaining tofu (see page 109).

You can replace the chocolate oat milk with any milk alternative and add 1 tablespoon of cocoa powder to it.

COCONUT CRISPY OATS

MAKES 1 CUP

1 cup gluten-free old-fashioned rolled oats
1 tablespoon coconut oil, melted (see Note)
2 tablespoons maple syrup
1 teaspoon ground cinnamon

Preheat the oven to 350°F.

In a medium bowl, toss the oats with the melted coconut oil, maple syrup, and cinnamon. Spread the oats out on a sheet pan. Bake in the oven, stirring them occasionally, for about 15 minutes, until they are brown and crispy.

The oats will keep for several weeks in a sealed container in your pantry.

NOTE No coconut oil? No problem! Use what you have on hand, such as olive oil or any vegetable oil.

ABC BREAKFAST TACOS

(AVOCADO BACON CHEESE)

SERVES 2

3 slices bacon, cut into julienne strips (see Note)

2 tablespoons olive oil or salted butter, for cooking the eggs

4 large eggs, whisked together

2 large ripe avocados, diced

6 small corn or flour tortillas

½ cup shredded jalapeño Jack cheese

Fresh herbs or arugula, for garnish

Charred Salsa Roja (page 271) or hot sauce of choice

NOTE Storing sliced bacon in the freezer allows you to julienne the very cold bacon into super-thin strips more easily than bacon at a refrigerated temperature. Just remove it from the freezer, wait a few minutes, and slice the amount you need. Return the remaining bacon to the freezer.

VEGAN OPTION Replace the eggs with scrambled soft silken tofu, adding fresh grated turmeric to color them yellow, and use crispy garbanzo beans (page 273) instead of the bacon.

Avocado toast is the toast of the town from coast to coast. Although we at Malibu Farm are Instagram central, we resisted putting it on our menu because it is a little too California millennial cliché, even for us. This breakfast taco is inspired by avocado toast. Also inspired by avocado toast: our avocado pizza (see page 247).

Don't eat bacon? Swap it out with beans for vegetarian taco dreams. And add sprouts if you wish, as it is your dish. For that matter, wrap the mixture up into a burrito package.

Heat a small skillet over medium heat until a drop of water evaporates on contact. Add the julienned bacon strips and cook until they are crispy, about 5 minutes. Drain the bacon on paper towels and set aside. (Discard the bacon fat, or save it to add smoky bacon flavor to sautéed potatoes or vegetables; you can also use the warm rendered fat instead of olive oil in any dressing recipe.)

Warm the oil or butter in a medium skillet over low heat, and add the eggs. Cook, stirring, until they are softly scrambled, and then gently stir in the bacon strips and diced avocado.

While the eggs are cooking, place the tortillas on a griddle or a large skillet over medium heat. (Depending on the size of your skillet, you may have to do this in batches.) Divide the cheese over the tortillas, and heat until the tortillas become warm and slightly crispy and the cheese begins to melt, about 2 minutes. Transfer the tortillas to a serving plate or platter. Top the tortillas with the scrambled egg mixture, and garnish with fresh herbs or arugula. Serve with Charred Salsa Roja or hot sauce alongside.

THE OPEN-FACE SALAD OMELET

SERVES 2

Olive oil blend

4 large eggs

½ cup shredded mozzarella cheese

1 cup halved cherry tomatoes

2 cups fresh arugula

Lemon dressing (recipe follows)

Salt to taste

2 tablespoons shaved Parmesan cheese, for garnish (optional)

4 slices prosciutto, for garnish (optional)

NOTE Wait, did I say to use a *nonstick* pan?! Well, I am neither a doctor nor a scientist, but I know that most nonstick pans no longer contain perfluorooctanoic acid (PFOA), which is a suspected carcinogen, and wowsy, those are two long words I don't use often. But most nonstick skillets available for purchase today are perfectly safe to use. Use whatever pan you are comfortable using.

One morning at 9 a.m. I wanted a salad. It seemed too early for a salad, but I was hungry. And so I made a very thin omelet, and I topped it with a very big salad. It was exactly what I wanted: a little bit of egg with my salad. I put it on the restaurant menu, and lo and behold, I am not the only one who wants a salad omelet.

This version is inspired by prosciutto arugula pizza, but you can top yours with your favorite salad. The omelet goes great with the Greek salad on page 213 or with the raw Brussels sprout salad in my first book, *Malibu Farm Cookbook,* page 66.

Two eggs are suggested here per serving, but you can use three egg whites, or one whole egg and two whites, or you can use an egg substitute. What I'm trying to say is, use whatever your egg preference is. We're making a super-thin open-face omelet, more like a crepe, so the size of your pan will determine the diameter and thickness of your omelet. I use a 6-inch skillet. Choose a pan that's lightweight enough to lift easily. If you are using a pan that is not nonstick, you will need more oil.

Oil a 6-inch nonstick skillet (see Note) and heat it over medium heat.

In a small bowl, whisk the eggs together. Pour half of the eggs into the skillet, and cook without stirring until the

(RECIPE CONTINUES)

omelet starts to brown and sizzle and is mostly cooked through, about 3 minutes. Sprinkle half of the mozzarella cheese over the omelet, cover the skillet with a lid, and cook for about 1 minute so the cheese melts. Transfer the omelet to a plate. Repeat with the remaining eggs and cheese to make a second omelet.

In a medium bowl, toss the cherry tomatoes with the arugula and the lemon dressing. Season with salt to taste, and top the omelet with the salad. Garnish with the shaved Parmesan cheese and prosciutto, if using.

SERIOUSLY CITRUS DRESSING

MAKES ABOUT ¾ CUP

Citrus dressing is my favorite thing and it goes with just about everything. Use limes or lemons for lime or lemon dressing. Or get creative—try grapefruit dressing in the fall and blood orange dressing in the winter. Always have some in your fridge, ready to go!

½ cup juice from any citrus: lemon, lime, orange, grapefruit

¼ cup olive oil

1 garlic clove, grated

Salt to taste

Chopped fresh herbs, such as parsley, cilantro, or rosemary (optional)

The key here is fresh-squeezed juice, not bottled. How much oil will you use? This all depends on how much juice you have squeezed, but you want to have more juice than olive oil, which is why we call it "seriously" citrus dressing.

Just whisk the citrus juice with the olive oil, stir in the garlic, and season with salt. Add chopped herbs if using. Voilà.

GREEN EGGS AND HAM

SERVES 2

3 ounces (about ½ cup) chopped dry chorizo (yes, you can replace the chorizo with cooked bacon, cooked sausage, or tofu)

¼ cup halved cherry tomatoes

½ cup cooked garbanzo beans (chickpeas), purchased or homemade, drained (see Note, page 273)

¼ cup Cubed Roasted Butternut Squash (page 54)

½ cup loosely packed fresh spinach leaves

¼ cup Tomatillo Salsa Verde (recipe follows)

4 large eggs

2 slices Havarti cheese

¼ cup Green Jalapeño Harissa (recipe follows)

A classic dish that originated in North Africa and the Middle East, shakshuka is traditionally made with a tomato base and poached eggs. This dish is inspired by shakshuka, and like that dish, it is served in (or from) a cast-iron skillet. You can use small individual skillets, as we do here, or triple the recipe and make this dish in a large cast-iron skillet or paella pan for a breakfast party serving six.

We use two green sauces for ours, but you do not need both. You can use one or the other, both, or something that's already in your fridge, such as Charred Salsa Roja (page 271).

Preheat the oven to 375°F.

Divide the chorizo between two individual cast-iron skillets, and cook it over medium heat for about 1 minute, until it begins to brown. Add the cherry tomatoes, garbanzo beans, butternut squash, and spinach, and heat for a few minutes. Stir in the Tomatillo Salsa Verde.

Cook the eggs your favorite way—fried, scrambled, or poached—and place them on top of the chorizo-veggie mixture in the skillets. Top each with a slice of Havarti cheese, and place the skillets in the oven for about 2 minutes, until the ingredients are hot and the cheese is melted. Top with the Green Jalapeño Harissa.

(RECIPE CONTINUES)

TOMATILLO SALSA VERDE

MAKES 1½ CUPS

4 tomatillos, husks discarded, chopped
½ medium white onion, chopped
1 garlic clove
Juice from 2 limes
½ cup fresh cilantro
2 avocados, peeled and seeded
Salt to taste

Place the tomatillos, onion, garlic, lime juice, cilantro, 1 avocado, and salt in a blender. Pulse until smooth. Transfer the puree to a small bowl. Chop the remaining avocado and stir it into the blended salsa. This salsa is fingerlickin' good, and you can really eat it with anything.

GREEN JALAPEÑO HARISSA

MAKES 1 CUP

2 limes
1 cup fresh parsley
½ bunch fresh cilantro
1 jalapeño pepper, chopped fine
2 teaspoons ground cumin
1 teaspoon ground coriander
⅓ cup olive oil
Salt to taste

Zest and juice the limes. Combine the lime zest and juice, parsley, cilantro, jalapeño, cumin, and coriander in a blender. Process until smooth. With the blender running, slowly add the oil. Season with salt. The harissa will last 3 to 5 days in the fridge.

NOTE Harissa is a Tunisian hot chile pepper paste, and there are many versions and variations, with different chilies, herbs, and spices.

SURFERS RANCHEROS

SERVES 2

5 tablespoons vegetable or avocado oil, to fry

4 small corn tortillas

1 small russet potato, peeled and chopped

Salt to taste

½ cup cooked black beans, purchased or homemade (drained and rinsed)

½ cup Cubed Roasted Butternut Squash (recipe follows)

½ red onion, sliced

½ red bell pepper, sliced

1 cup Charred Salsa Roja (page 271)

4 large eggs

1 cup shredded cabbage

1 avocado, sliced

¼ cup crumbled feta cheese

3 tablespoons sour cream

VEGAN OPTION Skip the egg, and add chopped tofu to the vegetables, drizzle with vegan sour cream (see page 109), and vegan cheese.

Huevos rancheros are a breakfast dish from Mexico, and the original version never goes out of style, but I am completely enamored with our Malibu take on the classic. It is conveniently made using our favorite ingredients: squash, potato, and beans. They have the comforting look of traditional rancheros but are lighter and brighter, celebrating a day at the beach.

Heat 3 tablespoons of the oil in a small skillet over high heat. One at a time, add the corn tortillas and fry until they are crispy, about 1 minute. Drain the tortillas on paper towels and, once cool, break into chips. (Did I say *fry?* Well, yes. I don't fry a lot, but tortilla chips are the exception to the no-frying rule, because all rules are meant to be broken occasionally for the right reason. Chips are always the right reason.)

Heat the remaining 2 tablespoons oil in a medium skillet over medium heat. Add the potato and sauté until the pieces are just crispy and cooked through, about 5 minutes. Season with salt and transfer to a medium bowl. Add the beans and the butternut squash to the potatoes. Cover the bowl to keep warm.

In the same medium skillet, sauté the red onion and red bell pepper together for about 3 minutes, until they begin to soften. Stir in the Charred Salsa Roja and heat it slightly. Set the skillet aside.

(RECIPE CONTINUES)

Finally, now that all your ingredients are prepared, cook the eggs your favorite way. There is no wrong way—fried, scrambled, over easy, or over hard, your eggs your way.

Place a generous spoonful of the potato/bean/squash mixture on each plate and top it with the fried tortillas. Arrange the eggs on top of the chips, and then spoon the salsa over the eggs. Top with the cabbage, avocado, and feta, and drizzle with the sour cream.

CUBED ROASTED BUTTERNUT SQUASH

MAKES ABOUT 4 CUPS
(DEPENDING ON THE SIZE OF THE SQUASH)

Butternut squash is one of my favorite ingredients. It is so versatile and we use it in many of our dishes for its beautiful color and touch of sweetness.

1 butternut squash, peeled, seeded, and chopped into medium (½-inch) or small (¼-inch) dice—either is fine

3 tablespoons olive oil

Salt to taste

3 tablespoons agave nectar or honey

Juice from 1 lemon

Preheat the oven to 400°F.

In a bowl, toss the chopped squash with the olive oil. Spread the squash cubes out on a sheet pan and roast in the oven until they are just soft and a little browned but not mushy, 15 to 20 minutes. Season with salt, and drizzle with the agave and lemon juice.

PYTT I PANNA

(SMOKED SALMON HASH)

SERVES 4

Olive or vegetable oil

2 medium russet potatoes, peeled and diced (3 cups)

Salt to taste

1 medium zucchini, diced (1 cup)

2 tablespoons diced onion

1 cup Cubed Roasted Butternut Squash (opposite page)

8 large eggs

½ cup Classic Marinated Roasted Beets (page 79; optional)

8 slices smoked salmon, chopped

Chopped fresh arugula and/or parsley, for garnish

Horseradish Cream (recipe follows)

This is a pretty traditional *pytt i panna* (literal translation: "mixed in the pan"), which is a potato hash with lots of goodies—veggies and salmon in this case, although in Sweden this dish is commonly made with sausage or other meat. You can substitute different ingredients from your fridge. Traditionally, it's a way of using leftovers. We top ours with fried eggs and horseradish cream, and it is a Swedish dream.

I like to cook all my ingredients separately so that each one is cooked just right. Start with the potatoes: Add about 2 tablespoons oil to a large skillet and heat it over medium heat. Add the potatoes and let them brown and crisp on one side, 3 to 5 minutes, before stirring to brown them on the opposite side, an additional 3 to 5 minutes. Season the potatoes with salt and transfer them to a bowl.

Add a little oil to the same skillet and sauté the zucchini in the same way, about 2 minutes. Season with salt and transfer the zucchini to the bowl containing the potatoes.

Finally, cook the onion in the same way for about 2 minutes, until just softened, and leave them in the skillet. Return the cooked potatoes and zucchini to the skillet, and gently stir in the roasted butternut squash. Heat through.

In a separate pan, fry, scramble, or poach the eggs per your preferred egg deliciousness.

(RECIPE CONTINUES)

Divide the hash among four plates. Add the beets (if using) and then the smoked salmon. (The beets tend to bleed all over the rest of the hash, which is why we add them next to last. Although you could skip the beets, they do add a nice acidic punch to the dish.)

Top the hash with the cooked eggs. Garnish with arugula or chopped parsley or both. Drizzle the Horseradish Cream over the top.

HORSERADISH CREAM

MAKES 1 CUP

Traditionally horseradish cream is made with crème fraîche or sour cream, but you can also use yogurt (vegan or regular). To make a thicker spread, switch with cream cheese and spread on bagels with lox. Delish. Additionally, you can substitute horseradish with wasabi.

1 cup crème fraîche or sour cream

1 tablespoon (or to taste) prepared horseradish (see Note)

2 tablespoons fresh lemon juice

Pinch of salt

In a small bowl, combine the crème fraîche or sour cream, horseradish, lemon juice, and salt. The cream will keep in the fridge for 3 days.

NOTE Can you make your own prepared horseradish? Yes, easy. Pick up a root from the market, or from your garden if you grew it. Peel off the skin, and chop the white root into medium pieces. Pulse in a food processor with a few tablespoons of water until it is a soft mash, then add a splash of distilled white vinegar and pulse again, and season with a pinch of salt. Careful—the fumes are hot, so don't breathe them in! Homemade prepared horseradish is spicy and delicious and lasts for a few weeks in the fridge.

TIPS Horseradish Cream is great with brisket (see page 229), with grilled steak or lamb, or drizzled on blanched green beans.

Make a horseradish vinaigrette with 1 tablespoon prepared horseradish, 2 tablespoons fresh lemon juice, 1 teaspoon honey, a dash of salt, 1 grated garlic clove, and ¼ cup olive oil.

VEGAN VEGGIE SCRAMBLE

WITH TOFU

SERVES 4

1 (14-ounce) package extra-firm tofu

Olive oil

Salt to taste

1 cup cherry tomatoes

2 cups Cubed Roasted Butternut Squash (page 54)

4 cups fresh baby spinach

NOTE We serve this as a vegan dish—but guess what? Guests often order it with eggs added, so go ahead and scramble some eggs into it if you wish. You can also use mashed silken soft tofu, with 1 tablespoon grated turmeric root for flavor and color, which makes it look like "real" eggs. Try both versions and tell me which you like best!

There are lots of vegan egg substitutes on the market, but my favorite vegan hot breakfast dish is tofu sautéed with squash, tomatoes, and spinach. Unless I am making a soft, long-simmered stew or soup, I prefer to cook my ingredients separately so that each one is cooked just right, and this recipe is no exception. We serve it with breakfast potatoes and salsa roja (page 271) or sweet and hot habanero sauce (recipe follows).

Start with the tofu: Drain the tofu and dry it well on paper towels. (Any water from the tofu that mixes with the oil in the pan can splatter into a gas flame, causing the flame to flare up.) Cut the tofu into ½-inch cubes; you should have 2 cups.

Heat 1 tablespoon oil in a large skillet over high heat, add the tofu cubes, and sauté until they are browned and crisp on one side. Then stir to crisp them on the second side, about 5 minutes total. Season the tofu lightly with salt, transfer it to a medium bowl, and set it aside.

In the same skillet, blister the cherry tomatoes by shaking the pan to brown them on all sides until the skin just begins to pop, about 2 minutes. Add the butternut squash and stir until it is heated through. Add the cooked tofu and the spinach, and combine for about 1 minute, until the spinach just begins to wilt. Serve while hot.

SWEET AND HOT HABANERO SAUCE

MAKES 8 CUPS

4 habanero chile peppers, or to taste

1 orange bell pepper

3 red bell peppers

1 tablespoon salt

¼ cup sugar

1 cup distilled white vinegar

1 mango, peeled and seeded (optional)

TIP Don't toss your leftover vinegar or oil bottles. Clean and reuse them by storing your hot sauce in one. You can also buy small 8-ounce swing-top bottles for this.

NOTE Sweeten the hot sauce with agave, honey, or maple syrup and use as a dip for monster sprouts (see page 189).

I always eat hot sauce with my eggs. Spice up your morning! So easy, so fast, so spicy, so amazing. We also use this hot sauce for our yellow tacos (see page 284).

When touching raw chile peppers, be careful, please, because getting chile oil in your nose or in your eyes is no fun at all. Safety first.

Remove the stems from the habanero chile peppers, but keep the seeds if you want extra heat. Remove the stems and seeds from the orange and red bell peppers, and coarsely chop the peppers. Combine all the peppers with the salt, sugar, vinegar, and mango (if using) in a blender, and process until smooth. When you open the lid of the blender, don't breathe in the fumes, as this could send you into a coughing fit. Also no fun.

Taste the sauce: For more spice, add more habanero peppers. For more sweetness, add more mango. This recipe makes a lot, but the sauce will last 2 weeks in the fridge in an airtight bottle. Got friends? Make them a bottle and give the hot gift that keeps on giving spice, meal after meal.

KALE APPLE SERRANO HOT SAUCE

MAKES 2 CUPS

1 or 2 apples (according to how hot you like your sauce), peeled, cored, and cut into pieces

4 serrano chile peppers

⅔ cup apple cider vinegar

¼ cup brown or white sugar

⅔ cup chopped fresh dinosaur (lacinato) kale

Pinch of salt

NOTE Sweeten the hot sauce with agave, honey, or maple syrup and use as a drizzle or dip for avocado pizza (page 247) or quesadillas (page 247).

One day it was obvious: we needed a green hot sauce. Why we had not thought of it before was a mystery. Welcome to the family, kale apple serrano hot sauce.

In a blender, combine 1 apple with the chiles, vinegar, brown sugar, kale, and salt. Process until smooth. Is it too spicy for you? Add the second apple until it is just right.

Allow the sauce to rest for 15 minutes, then remove and discard the foam that has accumulated on top. The hot sauce will last 2 weeks in the fridge in an airtight bottle (see Tip, opposite page).

MIDDAY LUNCH

My **FAVORITE LUNCH** is leftovers, a reminder of yesterday fueling the body today. I like to include components from the day before that can easily be assembled into a **QUICK AND HEALTHY MEAL**. Preparing lunch from scratch seems like a luxury. The time for that is not easily or often available, unless it is a **SPECIAL OCCASION**.

Lunch is **EAT AND GO**—hiking, swimming, running, surfing, working. Or it is **EAT AND GROW**—at school, at a lecture, at the movies, at a museum, through traveling, through volunteering. Or it is just **EAT AND SLOW**—rest, meditation, healing, self-reflection.

What is the **PERFECT LUNCH**? It can be alone or with others. It can be quick or it can be leisurely. It can be at work or at home. But a perfect lunch needs all the **MAGIC** components of the **SMORGASBORD OF MY DREAMS**: a green salad, a vegetable, a grain or a potato, and a little bit of protein, which could be beans or cheese or a small piece of fish or chicken.

Now that you know **WHAT I LIKE FOR LUNCH**, I am ready for my **INVITE**.

Léoube

MALIBU
FARM

VEGETABLE CRUST PIZZAS

SERVES 3

CAULIFLOWER CRUST

1 head cauliflower, or about 7 cups purchased cauliflower rice

½ cup shredded three-cheese blend (Monterey Jack, Colby, and Cheddar cheeses)

¼ cup grated Parmesan cheese

3 large eggs, beaten

3 tablespoons cornmeal

3 tablespoons almond meal

1 teaspoon salt

Olive oil

PIZZA TOPPINGS

Tomato sauce or pesto

Sliced fresh mozzarella cheese

Sliced heirloom tomatoes

FOR SERVING

Arugula tossed in lemon dressing (see page 48)

Finely shredded raw cauliflower or zucchini

The cauliflower crust pizza is the number one-selling menu item at all our locations. Although there is a plethora of recipes online, it took us many months to perfect this recipe. The softer the crust, the better it tastes—but then it falls apart when you try to eat it. The more stable you make it, the more it tastes like cardboard, which isn't what we want. Finding the right balance is the tricky part, and reproducing it in large batches as a restaurant can be very challenging. We learned that baking the shredded cauliflower was easier than steaming or microwaving it. The longer and higher temperature you bake it at, the drier it gets, which shrinks the yield, which is not ideal. So we bake it partially and then remove the excess liquid.

Once we finally mastered the cauliflower crust, we also made a zucchini crust, which is actually my favorite, and then I had some more crust ideas to try. Brussels sprouts, carrot, or black bean crust sounds delicious, right? But the cooks said, "Someone stop her, please," and so no more experiments were attempted.

We serve more than one thousand vegetable crust pizzas per week in Malibu. I'm sharing our cauliflower recipe here, and you can simply swap in 4 large zucchinis for a zucchini crust, or broccoli for a broccoli crust. Want to use other veggies? Try it and let me know how it turns out!

(RECIPE CONTINUES)

Preheat the oven to 325°F.

If you are using fresh cauliflower, shred it in a food processor or with a grater to make about 7 cups "rice." Spread the cauliflower rice in a ½-inch-thick layer on a rimmed sheet pan (if you spread the cauliflower too thin, it may brown too much, too fast). The cauliflower should almost fill a standard half-size sheet pan. Roast it in the oven for about 40 minutes, stirring it once. Do not over-roast it—the cauliflower should be mostly white, with about 25 percent of it showing light-brown spots.

Remove the sheet pan from the oven and let the cauliflower cool. It will have shrunk to about 4 cups during the roasting.

There are two options for removing the excess liquid at this point. You can place the roasted cauliflower in a perforated pan (such as a strainer) set over a bowl, cover it with a weight, and leave it in the refrigerator overnight. Or you can place it in a cheesecloth bundle and squeeze it until most of the liquid is released. Once you have removed the excess liquid, you will have about 2 cups of packed cooked cauliflower—yes, it is ever shrinking in size. Transfer the roasted and drained cauliflower to a mixing bowl, and stir in the three-cheese blend, Parmesan, eggs, cornmeal, almond meal, and salt until combined.

Raise the oven temperature to 375°F.

Divide your cauliflower "dough" into three 8-ounce balls. Then flatten each piece to resemble a hockey puck, drizzle a bit of oil over them, and place them on well-oiled sheet pans.

To form each pizza crust, cover a puck with a piece of parchment paper or plastic wrap, and press down on it with an 8-inch cake pan until a disk is formed. (You can press out the disk with your hands, but it is easier to make it smooth and even if you press it with a flat-bottom pan.)

TIP To make zucchini crusts, follow the same steps, grating 4 large zucchinis instead of the cauliflower. You can use these vegetable crusts with any of your favorite pizza toppings, such as pepperoni, sausage, or prosciutto.

Bake the crusts for about 15 minutes, rotating the sheet pans halfway through to ensure that they brown evenly. The crust is done when it is slightly brown around the edges and on the bottom. Be careful not to overbake the crusts, as the pizzas will be baked again once toppings are added.

The pizza crusts will keep for 1 week in the fridge. They can also be frozen if they are vacuum sealed.

To make pizzas, spread each crust with 2 tablespoons tomato sauce or pesto, 3 slices of fresh mozzarella, and 3 slices of heirloom tomato. Or choose your own favorite toppings. The uncooked pizzas can be assembled up to 6 hours in advance. Refrigerate until you are ready to bake them.

When you are ready to eat, place the pizzas on a sheet pan and bake them in a preheated 375°F oven for 7 minutes, or until the cheese is just melted.

To serve, we garnish our pizzas with arugula tossed in lemon dressing and finely shredded raw cauliflower or zucchini.

CHICKEN NACHO TORTILLA SALAD

SERVES 4

2 to 4 cooked chicken breasts, sliced or chopped, about 1 cup per person (this is a great way to use leftover roasted chicken)

1 cup cooked fresh corn

1 cup green beans or sugar snap peas, blanched

1 cup black beans, purchased or homemade, drained

½ cup shredded jalapeño Jack cheese

8 cups salad greens of your choice

1 cup halved cherry tomatoes

2 cups corn tortilla strips, fried, or purchased tortilla chips

½ cup red or green salsa dressing (recipes follow)

VEGAN OPTION For a vegan version of this salad, sub tofu for the chicken, skip the cheese, and use vegan sour cream (see page 109) or vegan mayo (see page 218) instead of the mayonnaise in either the red or the green dressing.

I have an obsession with salsa, one that is really out of hand. I am not only a salsaholic but also a chipaholic, and I find a way to eat both every day. It started with the nachos (see page 269), which of course I was eating daily. But then I wanted salad with my chips, and so I began adding a mountain of kale on top of my nachos, and then some chicken. One day someone looked at my nachos and asked what I was doing. That was when I realized I was trying to convert my nachos into a nacho salad. And here it is. We made this salad with the red salsa dressing for years, but after we created the green hot sauce, we switched to the green salsa dressing. Both recipes are included, so you choose: red or green?

In a large bowl combine the chicken, corn, green beans or sugar snap peas, black beans, jalapeño Jack cheese, salad greens, cherry tomatoes, and tortilla strips or chips. Add the salsa dressing, toss, and serve.

(RECIPE CONTINUES)

RED SALSA DRESSING

MAKES 1 CUP

¾ cup mayonnaise, purchased or homemade (see page 218)

¼ cup Charred Salsa Roja (page 271) or your favorite salsa

1 tablespoon Sriracha or other hot sauce (optional)

1 teaspoon salt

In a small bowl, whisk the mayonnaise into the Charred Salsa Roja. Add the Sriracha for additional heat if desired, and season with the salt. This dressing can be made several days in advance and stored in the fridge.

TIP Add mayo, aioli, or lemon dressing (see page 48) to any salsa, pesto, hummus, or sauce to make it into a dressing or spread.

GREEN SALSA DRESSING

MAKES 1 CUP

½ cup mayonnaise, purchased or homemade (see page 218)

1 teaspoon salt

½ cup Kale Apple Serrano Hot Sauce (page 61), or to taste

In a small bowl, whisk the mayonnaise and salt into the Kale Apple Serrano Hot Sauce until combined and smooth. This dressing can be made several days in advance and kept in the fridge.

GRILLED SALMON KALE NIÇOISE SALAD

SERVES 4

4 large hard-boiled eggs

¼ cup beet juice (optional, see Note)

6 cups fresh purple kale or greens of choice

½ cup Niçoise Olive Dressing (recipe follows)

4 fish fillets (salmon or other fish of choice), grilled or baked

2 cups green beans, blanched

8 baby potatoes, boiled until soft and then cut in half

1 bunch baby carrots, boiled or roasted until tender

1 cup halved cherry tomatoes

½ cup pitted kalamata olives

¼ cup capers, drained

Grated or spiralized beets, for garnish (optional)

NOTE Where will you get beet juice? Easy, grate a few tablespoons of raw beets on a box grater, and there will be enough juice with the shredded beets to color your eggs. Use the grated beets as a garnish, if you like.

To turn this into a vegetarian salad, replace the fish fillets with cauliflower steak (see page 107).

Niçoise is a classic salad, as au courant today as it was decades ago. It originated in Nice, France, and is traditionally made with canned tuna, tomatoes, hard-boiled eggs, and Niçoise olives. It is now served all over the world, even here in Malibu. We make ours a purple dream salad, with purple kale, purple pickled eggs, purple potatoes, and purple green beans—but you can use the ingredients that are available in your market. To choose sustainable fish, check out guides such as SeafoodWatch.org.

If you want to color the eggs purple, roll them in the beet juice for a few minutes until the exterior is purple but the interior of the egg is still white. Then cut them in half. Or you can skip this step and serve the eggs just the way they are.

In a large serving bowl, lightly toss the kale with some of the Niçoise Olive Dressing, and then arrange the eggs, fish fillets, green beans, potatoes, carrots, cherry tomatoes, olives, and capers over the greens. Garnish with grated or spriralized beets, if desired. (Got leftover olive dressing? Make black olive chicken salad by tossing it with shredded roasted chicken and lots of herbs and radicchio.)

(RECIPE CONTINUES)

TIP If you prefer a mayonnaise-free dressing for the salad, use the mahimahi black olive vinaigrette (page 112).

NIÇOISE OLIVE DRESSING

MAKES 2½ CUPS

¾ cup kalamata or Niçoise olives, pitted

2 shallots

¼ cup chopped fresh parsley

1 garlic clove

1 cup mayonnaise, purchased or homemade (see page 218)

½ cup fresh lemon juice

2 tablespoons olive oil

Salt (optional)

In a food processor, combine the olives, shallots, parsley, and garlic, and pulse a few times until coarsely chopped. (You can also chop by hand if you prefer. It is always better to under-process than to overprocess.)

Add the mayonnaise and pulse a few times. We want it to be speckled with small chunks of green and black—not an evenly mixed puree of questionable color. (At this point you have made black olive aioli, which you can use as a crudité dip, as a sauce on a fish sandwich, or as a potato dip—it is delicious.)

To turn your aioli into a dressing, place it in a small bowl and whisk in the lemon juice and olive oil until it is thinned as desired. Season with salt if needed. The dressing can be made several days in advance and stored, covered, in the fridge.

VEGAN CHOP SALAD

SERVES 4

2 cups chopped romaine lettuce

2 cups chopped fresh black kale (also called dinosaur kale or lacinato kale)

½ cup cooked quinoa or other grain (optional)

Classic Chop Dressing (recipe follows)

2 cups Cubed Roasted Butternut Squash (page 54)

1 cup Classic Marinated Roasted Beets (page 79)

2 avocados, sliced

2 cups halved cherry tomatoes

2 cups garbanzo beans (chickpeas), purchased or homemade, drained (see Note, page 273)

Watermelon radishes, sliced thin, for garnish (optional)

NOTE The butternut squash and the beets can both be made several days in advance.

The original cafe menu has barely changed since the opening of the pop-up in September 2013. Those dishes worked. There was never a reason to change the menu, with the exception of one dish: the chop salad.

The original menu had a classic chop salad with cheese, meat, and garbanzo beans (see my first book, *Malibu Farm Cookbook*, page 271). It was and is a delicious salad, but customers kept trying to modify it with more vegetables, asking for vegetables we did not have available.

We experimented with several different vegetables and finally settled on squash, which is sweet, and marinated beets, which are acidic, for our perfect combo. And better yet, both are available year-round. The new vegan salad was a winner. However, guests often add grilled chicken, fish, or steak to the "vegan" salad!

In a large bowl, toss the romaine, kale, and quinoa (if using) with the Classic Chop Dressing. Then layer the butternut squash, roasted beets, avocado slices, cherry tomatoes, garbanzo beans, and radishes (if using) decoratively on top.

(RECIPE CONTINUES)

NOTE Roasted sweet potatoes or carrots instead of squash? Of course! Black beans, lentils, quinoa instead of garbanzo beans? Yes, yes. Pickled jicama instead of beets? Go for it. Color this salad your favorite vegetable way.

CLASSIC CHOP DRESSING

MAKES ½ CUP

2 tablespoons Dijon mustard

6 tablespoons red wine vinegar

Salt to taste

1 small shallot, chopped fine (about 1 tablespoon)

½ cup (8 tablespoons) olive oil, canola oil, or a blend of the two

Of course you may use the recipe measurements to make your dressing, but my wish is for you to learn to make this time-honored dressing by sight and feel.

Spoon some Dijon mustard into a small bowl. It really does not matter how much, but let's say 2 heaping tablespoons. Thin it with red wine vinegar until it has the consistency of heavy cream. This is your ratio of mustard to vinegar. Season with salt and add the finely chopped shallot. Now slowly whisk in the oil to emulsify. I like my dressing to be roughly 50 percent oil and 50 percent vinegar because I like it highly acidic, but a more traditional ratio would be double (or more) oil to vinegar. It is your dressing, so do it the way that works best for you—add as much oil as you like. The dressing can be made several days in advance and stored in the fridge.

CLASSIC MARINATED ROASTED BEETS

SERVES 4

4 medium-size beets, any color, skin on

⅓ cup olive oil

Salt to taste

Dash of sugar

¼ cup red wine vinegar

¼ cup fresh lemon juice

½ shallot, chopped fine

A few tablespoons of chopped fresh herbs, such as parsley, dill, or chives

1 garlic clove, grated

NOTE To make a bright-colored beet hummus, add 1 tablespoon of marinated beets to 2 cups of hummus and blend; garnish with a drizzle of yogurt before serving.

TIP Don't like beets? Use raw chopped jicama instead and marinate in the same way.

You can use these beets in any recipe. Just add burrata and candied nuts (see page 131) for a great salad, or serve the beets with steamed green beans or asparagus (see my first book, *Malibu Farm Cookbook,* page 62). We use these beets in many recipes throughout this book, such as the Vegan Chop Salad (page 77) and Pytt i Panna (page 55).

Preheat the oven to 375°F.

Place the beets in a small ovenproof dish, drizzle them with a few tablespoons of the olive oil and a dash of water, and cover the dish with foil. Roast the beets in the oven until they are just soft, 45 minutes to 1 hour, depending on their size.

Allow the beets to cool, and then peel the skin off the beets by rubbing a paper towel over them or by rubbing them under running water. Chop them into a fine dice or slice them into whatever desired shapes. Place the beets in a small bowl and season them with salt and a tiny dash of sugar, and drizzle with the remaining oil. Add the red wine vinegar, lemon juice, shallot, herbs, and garlic, and toss. Marinate for 30 minutes before using. The marinated beets will keep for 1 week in the fridge.

THE 'BU BEEF BURGER

WITH BACON BALSAMIC ONION JAM

SERVES 4

4 beef burger patties

Salt and pepper to taste

4 slices Havarti cheese

4 brioche buns, toasted

4 tablespoons lemon aioli (see page 219)

2 cups fresh arugula

4 heaping tablespoons Bacon Balsamic Onion Jam (recipe follows)

NOTE At the cafe, we serve the burger with heirloom tomatoes, red onion slices, arugula, and a pepperoncini aioli. To make the aioli, use the black olive aioli that's described as the base of the Niçoise Olive Dressing on page 74, substituting pepperoncini for the olives.

We serve a ton of vegetable-crust pizzas and vegan chop salads. We serve mountains of kale. We also sell a lot of chicken burgers and beef burgers. There is competition in town, with vegan burger patties taking a bite out of the meat and poultry industry. But for now, this traditional beef burger still reigns supreme as our top seller.

Heat a grill or set a large sauté pan over high heat. Season the burger patties lightly with salt and pepper, and grill or sauté them to your desired doneness.

While the burgers are still on the barbecue or stovetop, place the Havarti cheese slices on top of them to melt.

Spread each bottom brioche bun with 1 tablespoon of the lemon aioli, and place a generous handful of arugula on the same bun. Place the burger on top of the arugula, spread 1 heaping tablespoon of the Bacon Balsamic Onion Jam on the patty, and set the top brioche bun on top.

(RECIPE CONTINUES)

TIP Got leftover bacon jam? Add to a grilled cheese sandwich. Or make a Turkey bacon jam club sandwich, with sliced turkey, lettuce, cheese, lemon aioli, and bacon jam. Or a spinach salad, with eggs and bacon jam vinaigrette, oh yes? Thin the jam with olive oil to make a dressing, warm it up, pour it on your greens, and lunch is served.

BACON BALSAMIC ONION JAM

MAKES 4 CUPS

½ pound sliced bacon, cut into julienne strips (see Note, page 45)

3 pounds white onions (3 to 4 onions), chopped fine

2 tablespoons sugar

¾ cup balsamic vinegar

In a large sauté pan, cook the bacon over low heat until the fat is rendered and the slices are lightly cooked, about 10 minutes. Add the onions and cook until they begin to sweat, about another 10 minutes. Add the sugar and balsamic vinegar, and cook for about 1 hour, stirring occasionally, until the jam is thick, sweet, sticky, salty, and addictive.

Bacon Balsamic Onion Jam will keep for 1 week in the fridge; reheat it before using.

LEMON SAFFRON PASTA FARM-ONARA

SERVES 2 TO 4

½ pound spaghetti (my favorite pasta brand is De Cecco; they have some organic varieties as well)

Salt to taste

1 cup heavy cream

A few strands of saffron

½ cup fresh lemon juice

2 garlic cloves, grated

2 egg yolks

½ cup grated Parmesan cheese, plus extra for garnish

Cracked black pepper to taste

3 slices bacon, cut into julienne strips, cooked until crispy, for garnish (see Note, page 45)

3 tablespoons chopped fresh parsley, for garnish (optional)

TIP Oh yes, you can use spaghetti squash instead of spaghetti. Or try hearts of palm linguini—so good. A serving of pasta is considered to be 2 ounces or 56 grams of cooked pasta per person; depending on how much pasta you like, this recipe serves up to four. Add a simple arugula salad with tomatoes and red wine vinaigrette (see page 78), and the meal is complete and plentiful.

Farm-onara = Farm Carbonara. This is a delightful cross between lemon pasta and pasta carbonara. You can use more bacon than the recipe calls for, but a little goes a long way. I love exaggerating colors, and I often use saffron with egg yolks to get the color to really shine. What else can you make with saffron and egg yolks? A gorgeous crème brûlée, of course (see page 145) or saffron ice cream (see my first book, *Malibu Farm Cookbook,* page 280).

Cook the spaghetti according to the package instructions in boiling water salted like the sea.

While the spaghetti is cooking, in a small pan stir the heavy cream with the saffron over low heat for about 5 minutes, until the saffron color and flavor are released. Let the mixture cool to room temperature, and then whisk in the lemon juice and garlic. Season to taste with salt, and finally whisk in the egg yolks.

When the spaghetti is cooked al dente, reserve ½ cup of the cooking water and drain the spaghetti. Return the spaghetti to the empty pot and immediately pour in the egg mixture and quickly stir the spaghetti around until the eggs are incorporated throughout. Now stir in the Parmesan cheese and taste for seasoning. If it is too thick, stir in the reserved spaghetti water to thin it. I am not usually a black pepper fan, but in this case, pepper away.

Transfer the spaghetti to a bowl, and top it with the cooked bacon strips, additional Parmesan cheese, and chopped parsley if using.

BEACH PICNIC POTATO SALAD

SERVES 4

Salt

2 pounds baby potatoes (do not peel; see Tips, page 88)

A few strands of saffron

Zest from 1 lemon plus 3 tablespoons lemon juice

1 garlic clove, grated

1 tablespoon whole-grain mustard (optional)

1 cup mayonnaise, purchased or homemade (see page 218)

1 bell pepper, any color, chopped fine

1 cup chopped fresh parsley or cilantro

½ red onion, sliced thin

1 celery stalk, sliced thin

TIP Add quinoa, lentils, or beans to your potato salads to up the nutritional and protein values. Sweet potato salad with black beans or orange lentils? Amazing. Or try white beans and white quinoa in the purple salad—so good. Yellow split peas and sauteed corn to saffron potato salad? Yes! The combinations are endless.

VEGAN OPTION Instead of regular mayo, use vegan mayonnaise, purchased or homemade (page 218).

I never saw a russet potato until I came to America. I thought all potatoes came in funky shapes and were cute little jewels. In Sweden, like most Swedes, we grew our own potatoes. As a child I anticipated the first early potato harvest the way other children anticipate Christmas. We would pick them when they were tiny, digging them up carefully so as not to bruise them, and then we would rush the deep-yellow Swedish Mandel potatoes (a.k.a. peanut fingerlings) from soil to stove, where we let them simmer in salted water.

Wines are known for their *terroir,* and how region, climate, and soil affect their flavor, but potatoes are the true underappreciated singers of the soil, and we tasted the past, present, and future in those diminutive potatoes. If I am feeling tired or sick, I don't reach for chicken soup; for me it's potatoes. This baby potato salad is one of my favorite ways to get my daily dose of vitamin Earth.

In a pot of salted boiling water, boil the potatoes until they are soft when pierced with a knife. The cooking time will vary depending on the size of your potatoes. Thanks to their long, skinny shape, baby fingerling potatoes cook a lot faster than a giant russet potato. Check the progress after about 10 minutes for babies and 25 minutes for larger potatoes. Drain and let them dry.

(RECIPE CONTINUES)

TIPS Always boil your potatoes with the skin on to prevent them from absorbing too much water. However, if you peeled the potatoes before cooking, drain them well and then make sure to dry them by returning them to the empty pot and warming them over low heat for a few minutes, or by placing them on a sheet pan and drying them in a 350°F oven for a few minutes. Wet potatoes don't make a good salad.

In the mood for a Southern-style potato salad? Add chopped hard-boiled eggs.

For a colorful salad, use boiled sweet potatoes tossed with the lime dressing on page 48, dill, and Fresno chile peppers (see page 113). Or for a more mysterious look, toss boiled Peruvian blue potatoes with Black Olive Vinaigrette (page 112) or niçoise dressing (page 74).

You can also substitute steamed cauliflower for the potatoes.

If your potatoes are babies, cut them in half. If they are bigger, you will need to cut them into smaller sizes. If you have a large russet, cut it in half lengthwise and then lay the cut side down, cut it in half again lengthwise, and then cut it crosswise four times. Say what? You lost me at "cut it lengthwise"?! All right, it is a potato salad, so cut the potatoes in any way and into any size you like. If you are using russets, you will need to peel them after you boil them.

Place the saffron strands in a large bowl, and pour 2 tablespoons of hot water over them to release their color and fragrance. Let them steep for a few minutes. Once the water has cooled, add the lemon zest and juice, garlic, mustard (if using), and mayonnaise, and stir until blended. Toss in the potatoes and taste for seasoning. Add more salt or lemon juice if needed. Add the bell pepper, parsley, red onion, and celery. This potato salad can be made several days in advance and stored in the fridge.

CHEESE-CORN-BACON PANINI

SERVES 2

2 ears fresh corn

4 slices bacon, cut into julienne strips (see Note, page 45)

4 slices jalapeño Jack cheese or Havarti cheese

4 slices country wheat bread or your favorite bread

4 tablespoons lemon aioli (see page 219), or 1 tablespoon vegetable oil plus 1 tablespoon salted butter

TIP You can use cooked chopped broccoli or butternut squash, sliced summer tomatoes, or steamed asparagus instead of the corn.

Not everything you make has to be smart, clever, or trendy. Sometimes we just want to eat. Food can be art and a chef can be an artist, but at its core food is fuel, and cooking is a craft honed through practice and repetition. Sometimes we may want to get creative in the kitchen, and sometimes we just want bread with cheese, and there is no shame in that. The best of times often include the simplest of foods.

At the cafe we serve the simplest form of the panini—country wheat bread with Havarti cheese—and I never get tired of this most basic sandwich. Tomatoes, bacon, and avocado are available as extras. At the restaurant we kick up a summer note by adding corn and bacon. Yes, please. Spreading the exterior of the bread slices with lemon aioli adds more crunchy deliciousness. The aioli will disappear as the bread cooks and only a hint of its flavor will remain.

You can of course use turkey bacon or vegan bacon or skip the bacon altogether and use black beans instead, which is just as delish.

To keep your corn nice and crisp, drop it in a pot of boiling water for 1 minute and then out it comes. Is it done? Yes, of course it is done. Corn can be eaten raw, so there is no need to cook it into mush. Drain it well.

(RECIPE CONTINUES)

Cook the bacon in a skillet over medium heat until the julienne strips are browned and crispy, about 2 minutes. Drain them on paper towels. (You can also bake your bacon in a 375°F oven for about 10 minutes until crispy.)

Layer the cheese, bacon, and corn on two slices of country bread, and top them with the other slices of bread. If you are using the lemon aioli, spread it over the exterior of the bread, and sauté the paninis in a skillet over medium heat until they are browned and crispy on both sides. If you are not using the aioli, add the oil and butter to the skillet and sauté the paninis over medium heat. The paninis can be assembled up to 2 days in advance.

CHEESE-CORN-BACON PANINI
(page 89)

BEACH PICNIC POTATO SALAD
(page 86)

CUCUMBER LIME GAZPACHO
(page 117)

POKE'VICHE

SERVES 2

1 pound sushi-grade fish (tuna, yellowtail, or salmon), chopped fine

1 tablespoon thinly sliced red or yellow onion

1 cup chopped sea asparagus, or super-thin slices of conventional asparagus

1 teaspoon toasted sesame seeds

Red chili flakes to taste

1 tablespoon soy sauce, or to taste

1 teaspoon toasted sesame seed oil (see Tip)

White jasmine rice, cooked (optional)

Freshly squeezed lime juice (optional)

TIP For an additional use of sesame seed oil, see Tip, page 206.

A short time after opening the casual counter-service cafe at the end of the pier, I was offered the opportunity to create a poolside cafe at the Four Seasons hotel in Manele Bay on the Hawaiian island of Lanai. I crossed the Pacific and took our simple concept from the funky Malibu Pier to a five-star Hawaiian resort. It was scary, thrilling, and amazing, but when new situations arise, all we can do is be who we are and do what we do and hope to accomplish the task.

Almost all of our locations are next to Nobu restaurants, which are of course premier Japanese restaurants specializing in raw seafood. Customers comment that when they want raw fish they go to Nobu, and when they want vegetables they come to Malibu Farm. But we've found success with this hybrid between a poke and a ceviche from our Lanai operation, created by Chef Ernest Lopez, and it's super-easy to make at home. All you need is really fresh sushi-quality fish (to choose sustainable fish, check out guides such as SeafoodWatch.org). We pair ours with taro chips, but any chip would work. We often serve this poke'viche in coconut halves, because how cute is that?

In a medium bowl, toss the fish, onion, sea asparagus, sesame seeds, red chili flakes, soy sauce, and sesame seed oil together. Season to taste with additional soy sauce.

To serve, can you put this on rice and call it a poke? Yes, you can. Can you squeeze in some lime juice and call it a ceviche? Yes, you can.

BEET IT, JUST BEET IT

SERVES 4

2 large chioggia (candy cane) beets (or any color)

2 tablespoons olive oil

Raw Beet Dressing (recipe follows)

3 tablespoons chopped fresh herbs (parsley, dill, or cilantro, or a mix of these herbs) or edible flowers

TIP This beet salad goes great with crumbled blue, goat, or burrata cheese.

TIP I love fig balsamic vinegar. If you can find it, use it.

They say less is more, but sometimes more is more, and in this case we are going to make a roasted beet salad with a raw beet dressing because beets with more beets is more fun.

Preheat the oven to 375°F.

Place the beets in a small baking dish and drizzle them with a few tablespoons of olive oil and a dash of water. Cover the dish with foil and roast the beets until they are just soft. This will take 45 minutes to 1 hour, depending on their size. Allow the beets to cool and then peel off the skin by rubbing the beets with a paper towel or by rubbing them under running water.

Slice the beets and arrange them on a platter. Pour the Raw Beet Dressing over the sliced beets. Garnish with herbs or edible flowers.

RAW BEET DRESSING

MAKES 1 CUP

½ cup peeled and shredded raw beets, any color

½ cup fig balsamic vinegar, cherry balsamic vinegar, or regular balsamic vinegar

1 garlic clove, grated

1 tablespoon finely chopped shallot (1 small shallot)

⅓ cup olive oil

Salt to taste

In a medium bowl, whisk together the shredded raw beets, vinegar, garlic, and shallot. Then slowly whisk in the oil and season with salt. This dressing will keep for 3 to 5 days in the refrigerator.

SUMMER TOMATO SALAD

BEET IT, JUST BEET IT (page 94)

COLOSSAL CARROTS WITH CARROT LIME DRESSING (page 98)

SUMMER TOMATO SALAD

SERVES 4

3 large yellow (or any color) heirloom tomatoes, thickly sliced

Yellow Beet Dressing (recipe follows)

3 tablespoons chopped fresh herbs (parsley, dill, or cilantro, or a mix of these herbs) or edible flowers

NOTE I use Meyer lemons, straight from my trees, which are super juicy; you may need to squeeze more lemons if you use another variety.

When it rains it pours, and when tomato season arrives the harvest bounty overflows with the most amazing selection of heirloom and cherry tomatoes. So many tomatoes, so many ways to eat them. I love this yellow beet dressing, which is both sweet and tart.

Arrange the sliced tomatoes on a platter, pour the dressing over them, and garnish with the herbs.

YELLOW BEET DRESSING

MAKES 1 CUP

½ cup peeled and shredded raw yellow beets

½ cup freshly squeezed lemon juice (about 2 lemons)

2 teaspoons Dijon mustard

2 teaspoons agave nectar

1 garlic clove, grated

½ cup olive oil

Salt to taste

In a medium bowl, whisk together the shredded yellow beets, lemon juice, Dijon mustard, agave, garlic, and oil. Season to taste with salt. This dressing will keep for 3 to 5 days in the fridge.

COLOSSAL CARROTS

WITH CARROT LIME DRESSING

SERVES 4

4 long, thick carrots, sliced into ¼-inch-thick rounds (see Tip)

3 tablespoons olive oil

Salt to taste

Carrot Lime Dressing (recipe follows)

3 tablespoons chopped fresh herbs (parsley, dill, or carrot tops, or a mix of these herbs) or edible flowers

TIP If you have carrot tops, make carrot top pesto instead of discarding them (see page 116). Carrot tops are also a great substitute for parsley as a garnish.

I used to fuss over my perfectly manicured garden beds, especially the baby vegetables, and I would feed giant overgrown vegetables to Arnold the pig. But one day I realized that bigger is better for me as well as for Arnold. Now, instead of using baby carrots served whole, I slice thick carrots into rounds, roast them, and serve them with this raw Carrot Lime Dressing. Yum, yum.

Preheat the oven to 375°F.

Spread the carrot rounds on a sheet pan and drizzle with the oil. Roast in the oven, turning them over once, for about 10 minutes or until they are just beginning to brown and soften. Remove from the oven and season lightly with salt.

To serve, place the roasted carrot slices on a plate and pour the Carrot Lime Dressing on top. Garnish with the herbs.

CARROT LIME DRESSING

MAKES ¾ CUP

½ cup shredded raw carrot

1 tablespoon agave nectar, honey, or maple syrup

Juice from 2 limes

¼ cup chopped fresh cilantro

1 garlic clove, grated

1 jalapeño pepper, or to taste, diced fine

3 tablespoons olive oil

1 teaspoon salt, or to taste

In a medium bowl, combine the shredded carrot with the agave, lime juice, cilantro, garlic, jalapeño, olive oil, and salt. Whisk together, and taste for seasoning. Adjust with additional jalapeño or salt as desired. This dressing will keep for 3 days in the refrigerator.

RAINBOW PEARL COUSCOUS

WITH ROMANESCO

SERVES 4

1 head Romanesco or cauliflower

2 tablespoons olive oil

2 cups pearl couscous (Israeli couscous)

Salt to taste

½ cup lemon dressing (see page 48)

1 cup fresh arugula or chopped herbs

NOTE The couscous can be cooked several days in advance, but the cauliflower is best when roasted right before using.

TIP When preparing cauliflower or broccoli, save the core! Slice it thin with a mandoline, use raw or sauteed, and toss with lemon dressing, lentils, and arugula. The core is, after all, the heart of the vegetable.

One of my favorite ways to increase my vegetable intake is by combining a starch or grain with 50 percent vegetables, such as broccoli mashed potatoes (see my first book, *Malibu Farm Cookbook,* page 68), Delicata Squash with Red Lentils (page 104), or Holiday Healthy Grains (page 239). Lately, one of my favorite combos has been this roasted Romanesco with pearl couscous.

Create a sunshine effect by cooking your couscous in saffron-infused water and substituting orange cauliflower (a hybrid variety sometimes called Cheddar Cauliflower) for the Romanesco. Or for a dish of purple dreams, use the hybrid 'Depurple' cauliflower and toss the cooked couscous in a little beet juice. Whatever the color, this dish goes great with any protein, such as fish, steak, chicken, or grilled tofu.

Preheat the oven to 400°F.

Break the Romanesco or cauliflower head into 1-inch pieces, and spread them out on a sheet pan. Drizzle with the oil. Roast for 10 minutes, or until the pieces are lightly charred and beginning to soften but still retain some crunch.

Meanwhile, cook the pearl couscous according to the package directions and then drain it.

Once the Romanesco is roasted and the pearl couscous is cooked, toss them together in a bowl and season with salt. Stir in the lemon dressing, and toss in the arugula or herbs.

DELICATA SQUASH

WITH RED LENTILS

SERVES 4

2 delicata squashes

Olive oil

1 cup red lentils, cooked according to the package directions and drained (see Note)

Salt to taste

2 tablespoons honey or agave nectar

¼ cup lemon dressing (see page 48)

Chopped fresh arugula, carrot tops, or herbs of choice, a little or a lot

1 serrano or Fresno chile pepper, pickled and sliced thin (see page 113; optional)

TIP Save the scooped-out squash seeds, rinse them and dry them, then roast them and eat them.

NOTE The lentils can be cooked several days in advance. Mix leftover lentils with rice (see Note, page 210) or add them to any salad. For example, substitute lentils for garbanzo beans in the Vegan Chop Salad (page 77) or the Raw Artichoke Salad (page 194).

Delicata is one of my favorite squashes. Unlike other squashes, such as pumpkin or kabocha, which are difficult to cut, the delicata, as its name suggests, is delicate and easy to slice when raw. Once this squash is cooked, the skin is easily digestible. My favorite way to serve it is roasted with red lentils, along with fresh herbs or salad greens. Sometimes I turn this dish into a salad with lots of greens, and other times it's more of a vegetable dish with just a garnish of greens.

Preheat the oven to 375°F.

Without removing the skin, clean the delicata squashes and cut them in half. Remove the seeds (see Tip) and cut the squashes into wedges. Place the squash pieces on a rimmed sheet pan and drizzle them with a few tablespoons of oil. Roast in the oven for 15 to 20 minutes, turning the wedges once, until they are lightly browned.

Remove the sheet pan from the oven and pour the drained cooked lentils over the squash. Season with salt, the honey, and the lemon dressing, and toss until well combined. Toss in the arugula, carrot tops, or herbs, and transfer the mixture to a large bowl or platter. Add the pickled chile pepper if using.

This salad can be eaten either warm or at room temperature, and it makes a great buffet dish.

THE BIG STEAK: CAULIFLOWER

WITH RED OR GREEN CHIMICHURRI

SERVES 2

1 head cauliflower

Salt to taste

Olive oil

½ cup lemon dressing (see page 48)

Green Chimichurri (recipe follows)

Red Chimichurri (recipe follows)

Tofu Sour Cream (recipe follows)

NOTE Chimichurri is an Argentinian sauce, with fresh herbs, garlic, oil vinegar, and often chiles. It is similar to a pesto but is nut and cheese free, which makes it a perfect condiment that is both vegan and without nut allergens.

What is your take on steak? Are you ready for a new kind of steak that is super easy to make? This cauliflower steak is paired with a bright green or red chimichurri and vegan sour cream, but if you're in the mood for something else, try Miso Tahini Sauce (page 206), vegan yogurt dressing (page 277), or Black Olive Vinaigrette (page 112). You can also sub broccoli for the cauliflower.

You can make your "steak" small or large. If you like a *big* steak, cut the cauliflower in half vertically, making a half head per person. That is usually too large for me, so I cut off the ends and reserve those for another use, such as faux potatoes (see page 118), and cut out two 1-inch-thick steaks from the center of the head.

Once you have the cauliflower steaks cut into the desired size, simmer them in a large pot of salted water until they are just cooked through not mushy. If you are using half heads of cauliflower, this will take about 20 minutes. If you have cut it into 1-inch-thick slices, it will take about 8 minutes. It is better to undercook than to overcook. If in doubt, take it out and let it drain. You can prepare it to this point as much as 2 days in advance.

If you are using sliced cauliflower, lightly oil a large skillet, warm it over high heat, and sear the slices until they are charred on both sides, 3 to 5 minutes per side. (You may have to do this in batches.)

(RECIPE CONTINUES)

If you are using halves, the top will be too round to sear in a skillet. Instead, preheat the broiler, place the halves flat-side down on a baking sheet, and drizzle a little oil over the top. Broil until the halves are nice and charred all over.

You can also put either type of steak on a barbecue grill or in a 400°F oven to roast for about 10 minutes. Like a steak made from beef, it is more appealing with a nice brown crust.

Once the cauliflower is charred, season it with salt and pour the lemon dressing over it. Serve the "steaks" with your choice of green or red chimichurri and vegan sour cream.

TIP Substitute kale, spinach, or other greens for the arugula.

GREEN CHIMICHURRI

MAKES 1 CUP

2 cups fresh arugula

2 tablespoons capers with 2 tablespoons caper juice

¼ to ½ teaspoon red chili flakes

¼ cup chopped fresh parsley

1 garlic clove

¼ cup olive oil, plus more if needed

Combine the arugula, capers and juice, chili flakes, parsley, garlic, and olive oil in a food processor and blend until the mixture reaches the consistency of pesto. Add more oil if needed. The sauce will last 3 days in the fridge.

TIP Guess what? Both the red and the green chimichurri sauces go great with The *Real* Big Steak (page 224). Or you could toss cooked baby potatoes with leftover chimichurri—yum.

RED CHIMICHURRI

MAKES 1 CUP

1 small red bell pepper, chopped

1 small ripe tomato

1 tablespoon pickled Fresno chile peppers (see page 113), plus 3 tablespoons pickle liquid

2 tablespoons chopped fresh parsley

1 small garlic clove

½ teaspoon salt

Combine the bell pepper, tomato, pickled chiles and pickle liquid, parsley, garlic, and salt in a food processor and blend until just combined but not over-blended. The sauce will last 3 days in the fridge.

TIP Leftover silken tofu? Make vegan pancakes (page 39) or a breakfast scramble (page 59).

NOTE To make vegan mayonnaise, see page 218.

TOFU SOUR CREAM

MAKES 1 CUP

Great for creamy vegan options, and super-quick and easy to make. I add a little sugar to mimic the sweetness of dairy. Use the tofu sour cream to create creamy vegan dressings, such as green or red salsa dressing (see page 72) or black olive vinaigrette (see page 112).

¾ cup silken (soft) tofu (see Tip)

2 tablespoons fresh lemon juice

1 tablespoons seasoned rice vinegar

½ teaspoon grated garlic

½ teaspoon sugar

Pinch of salt

Drain the tofu from the package and dry on paper towels. Then combine the tofu, lemon juice, vinegar, garlic, sugar, and salt in a food processor and blend until smooth. The vegan sour cream will keep for 3 to 5 days in the refrigerator.

MAHIMAHI

WITH BLACK OLIVE VINAIGRETTE

SERVES 4

2 pounds mahimahi fillets or other fish of your choice

Salt to taste

3 tablespoons lemon aioli (see page 219) or mayonnaise, purchased or homemade (see page 218)

Black Olive Vinaigrette (recipe follows)

VEGAN OPTION For a vegan version of this recipe, swap the fish for grilled tofu and use vegan mayonnaise.

Mahimahi is a firm, lean, white warmwater fish and is currently on the sustainable list (see SeafoodWatch.org). I am no expert, but I suppose that with ocean temperatures rising, warmwater fish is more likely to remain a stable population than coldwater fish. The sustainable seafood list will keep changing, but this sauce will work with any fish on the list.

Mahimahi can be grilled, broiled, or sautéed. Just keep it slightly undercooked, as it can quickly become dry if cooked too long. But wait—no worries if you overcook it accidentally! We will smother it in delicious Black Olive Vinaigrette, and you will never know.

Season the mahimahi fillets lightly with salt on both sides, and spread the lemon aioli over the fillets. (Coating lean fish with a light layer of aioli or mayonnaise helps lock in moisture and makes the fish less likely to stick to the grill.)

Cook on a barbecue grill or sauté in a large skillet over medium heat for about 10 minutes, depending on the thickness of the fillets, until just cooked through. The aioli or mayo is a substitute for oil and will burn off during the cooking process. Place the grilled fish on a serving platter and pour the dressing over it.

(RECIPE CONTINUES)

NOTE Feel free to use your favorite olive varieties in this recipe. You can also mix and match different olives and include capers and/or caper berries as well. Use leftover dressing with cauliflower steak (see page 107), for a purple potato salad (see page 86), or as a substitute dressing for salmon niçoise salad (see page 73).

BLACK OLIVE VINAIGRETTE

MAKES 2 CUPS

1 cup pitted kalamata olives (see Note), chopped

¼ cup lemon dressing (see page 48)

2 tablespoons chopped red onion

¼ cup chopped fresh herbs (rosemary, parsley, cilantro, or other herbs of choice)

2 tablespoons Fresno chile peppers, fresh or pickled (see opposite; optional)

Salt

In a bowl or jar, combine the olives, lemon dressing, onion, herbs, and chile (if using), and season with salt to taste. The dressing can be made as much as 4 days in advance.

PICKLED FRESNO CHILE PEPPERS

REAL OR FAKE?

MAKES 2 CUPS

1 cup white wine vinegar or rice vinegar

2 tablespoons salt

⅓ cup sugar

4 garlic cloves, sliced thin

2 star anise pods (optional)

1 tablespoon whole black peppercorns

6 Fresno chile peppers, sliced thin (see Note)

NOTE Although the Fresnos are not that hot, always be careful when you handle the seeds. Don't rub your nose or your eyes when working with any chile pepper. You can also substitute your favorite chile variety—red jalapeño, serrano, shishito—for the Fresno chile peppers.

TIP You can reuse the brine several times, so go ahead and add more chiles to the same brine after you finish the first batch. For more pickle options, use onions or carrots in the brine. For a less acidic brine, add ½ cup cold water to the mixture.

Pickled Fresno chile peppers are amazing on and with pretty much everything—and I want them on or with pretty much everything. But sometimes I don't feel like making them, so I may fake them instead. Here are instructions for whichever mood you're in.

MAKE 'EM

In a small pot, bring the vinegar to a light boil. Add the salt, sugar, garlic, star anise pods (if using), and peppercorns. Stir until the salt and the sugar have dissolved. Remove the pot from the heat and allow the mixture to cool to room temperature.

Stir the chile pepper slices into the vinegar mixture, and then transfer the contents to a jar or other container. The chiles will be ready to use after 12 hours in the brine and will keep in the fridge for as long as 1 month.

FAKE 'EM

All right, I must admit I often cheat when I make my pickled Fresno chile peppers. If you are faint of heart, close your eyes and cover your ears. I always have a jar of store bought cucumber pickles in my fridge, and I just slice up a couple of Fresno chile peppers and place them in the jar with the pickles. Presto, now my cucumber pickles get a spicy punch and I have pickled Fresno chile peppers, but all I had to do was slice them. Shh, don't tell.

CHICKEN PARM FROM THE FARM

SERVES 4

4 chicken breast cutlets

Salt to taste

1 cup lemon dressing (see page 48)

¼ cup kalamata olives, pitted

4 slices pancetta, for garnish (optional)

Olive oil

1 large heirloom tomato, sliced

¼ cup Carrot Top Pesto (recipe follows) or regular basil pesto, purchased or homemade

1 large ball of fresh mozzarella cheese, sliced

2 cups fresh arugula

¼ cup shaved Parmesan cheese, for garnish

NOTE Use your favorite olives—kalamata is simply a suggestion. Substitute sun-dried tomatoes for the pancetta if you don't eat pork.

The white meat chicken paillard, which is less glamorously called "chicken cutlet," makes a quick and light chicken Parmigiana with sliced heirloom tomatoes, pesto, mozzarella cheese, and kalamata olives. We serve it with arugula salad topped with crispy pancetta and Parmesan cheese.

Season the chicken breast cutlets lightly with salt on both sides, toss them with about ¼ cup of the lemon dressing, and let them sit in the refrigerator for up to 2 hours to marinate.

While the chicken is marinating, use a blender or food processor to combine and blend the olives with about 5 tablespoons of lemon dressing, creating a thick black olive spread.

Preheat the oven to 375°F.

If you are using the pancetta, place the slices on a sheet pan and roast in the oven until they are crispy, 5 to 8 minutes. Transfer to paper towels to drain.

On a grill or in a sauté pan brushed with 1 tablespoon of olive oil, cook the chicken over medium heat for about 5 minutes per side, or until just cooked through. Top each chicken cutlet with 1 slice of tomato, 1 tablespoon of pesto, and 1 slice of mozzarella cheese. Place them in the oven and bake for about 5 minutes, until the tomato is heated through and the cheese is beginning to melt.

(RECIPE CONTINUES)

To serve, place the chicken on individual plates or a platter. In a bowl, toss the arugula with the remaining lemon dressing, and place the salad on top of the chicken. Drizzle the plate with the black olive spread. Garnish with the crispy pancetta if using, and top with the Parmesan cheese.

CARROT TOP PESTO

MAKES 1 CUP

Carrot tops are totally underappreciated garden beauties, mostly cut off and discarded. They make great pesto, but don't stop there: substitute carrot tops for the arugula in the chimichurri recipe (see page 108), and use them as a garnish or anywhere instead of parsley.

1 cup loosely packed fresh carrot tops
⅓ cup shredded raw carrot
⅓ cup salted roasted cashews
1 small garlic clove
Juice from 1 lemon (about 4 tablespoons)
⅓ cup olive oil
1 teaspoon salt

Combine the carrot tops, shredded carrot, cashews, garlic, lemon juice, olive oil, and salt in a food processor and blend until the mixture forms a medium-smooth paste.

Use this as a substitute in any recipe that calls for pesto. Unlike basil, carrot tops stay green through heat and oxidation, and the pesto will keep for 5 days in the fridge.

NOTE This pesto would be a great accompaniment to vegan dishes, such as cauliflower steak (see page 107) and vegan potato salad (see page 86), or with pasta.

CUCUMBER LIME GAZPACHO

SERVES 2 TO 4

3 Persian cucumbers, chopped into a medium dice

2 tablespoons chopped red onion

1 cup fresh cilantro

2 tablespoons olive oil

¼ cup fresh lime juice (from about 2 limes), or to taste—tart is smart, but you may like less

Salt and pepper to taste

½ cup buttermilk (see Note)

I can and will eat tomato sandwiches all summer long. I will toss cherry tomatoes into my pasta, I will have tomatoes with mozzarella cheese, and I will make fresh salsa for every meal. But I will not make tomato soup, because as much as I love tomatoes, I do not love cold tomato soup. Tomato gazpacho makes me wish it was a salsa with chips instead of a cold soup. Cucumber gazpacho is more my style: refreshing crunch, with the punch of cilantro and lime.

This recipe is chop, chop, into the blender, whirl, whirl, and done. It takes all of 5 minutes to make. The soup will keep in the fridge for 3 days and is a great beach picnic soup.

NOTE Make ricotta cheese with your leftover buttermilk! Combine 2 cups of buttermilk with 4 cups of whole milk and 1 teaspoon salt in a small pot, and simmer for 5 minutes or until you see bubbles forming at the edges. Do not stir—let it bubble away on its own. Turn off the heat and allow the pot to rest on the stove for 10 minutes. Then use a slotted spoon to gently lift the curds into a strainer, and you've got about 2 cups of homemade ricotta cheese.

When you make cheese this way, there will be leftover water with proteins, minerals, and seasoning, also known as whey. Save it! Soak nuts or grains in whey for a boost of flavor, use in it in place of stock or water in a soup recipe, or substitute for water when you bake bread or pizza dough (page 254).

Prep the ingredients, but before you toss it all in the blender, reserve 3 tablespoons altogether of the cucumber, red onion, and cilantro. We are going to make a garnish similar to a pico de gallo. Chop the reserved cucumber, onion, and cilantro into a fine dice, place in a small bowl; add 1 tablespoon of the oil and a splash of the lime juice, season with salt, and set side.

Now go ahead, put the remaining cucumber, onion, and cilantro in a blender. Add the remaining 1 tablespoon oil, remaining lime juice, and the buttermilk, and whirl and blend but take it easy. Overprocessing is never a good thing. Blend until all the ingredients are just incorporated, leaving the soup a little chunky. Depending on the size of your Persian cucumbers, the soup may be too thick; if it is, thin it as desired with water, probably about ½ cup. Taste for seasoning, and add salt and pepper as needed. Pour the gazpacho into small glasses or a beach thermos, garnish with the reserved finely chopped veggies, raise your glass, and bottoms up. *Skål,* as we say in Sweden. Get drunk on your vegetables.

FAUX PARMESAN CAULIFLOWER "POTATOES"

SERVES 4

Salt to taste

1 head cauliflower, chopped (about 5 cups)

2 tablespoons salted butter

¼ cup crème fraîche (see Note)

5 tablespoons grated Parmesan cheese

2 tablespoons olive oil

3 garlic cloves, sliced thin

1 tablespoon chopped fresh rosemary

NOTE What is the difference between crème fraîche and sour cream? Crème fraîche has a higher fat content. Relax, that's a good thing: its fat content makes crème fraîche more suitable for heating, as it is less likely to separate. So use crème fraîche for hot or cold applications and sour cream for cold.

I live for broccoli mash, which is half broccoli and half potatoes, but this cauliflower dish is a total smash with no potatoes. It can easily be made in advance and just popped in the oven before serving. I like to keep the color of this mash really white so it resembles potatoes, so I boil the cauliflower, but you can also roast it, which will make the mash sweeter.

Preheat the oven to 450°F.

Bring a large pot of salted water to a boil, add the cauliflower, and boil until it is just soft, 5 to 8 minutes. Not super soft, not falling-apart mushy, just soft. Drain it well and add it to a food processor, along with the butter, crème fraîche, and 2 tablespoons of the Parmesan cheese. Process until smooth. Season with 2 teaspoons salt or to taste.

Warm the oil in a small skillet over medium heat, add the garlic, and sauté until it is just browned, about 2 minutes. Be careful not to burn it. Stir the garlic and the oil into the cauliflower mash. Transfer the mash to an ovenproof serving dish and sprinkle the remaining 3 tablespoons Parmesan cheese on top, along with the rosemary. The mash can be made to this point 1 day in advance and kept in the fridge.

Bake the mash in the oven until it is warm throughout and brown and crispy on top, yum yum. How long will this take? If you are making it fresh and the mash is still warm, it will take only 5 to 8 minutes to brown the top. But if the mash has been chilled overnight, it will take 12 to 15 minutes. It is done when it is warm and brown and crispy!

RATATOUILLE BOATS

SERVES 4

2 large eggplants

Olive oil

2 zucchinis, diced

1 bell pepper, any color, diced

¼ cup diced red onion

1 basket cherry tomatoes, halved (about 2 cups)

Salt to taste

2 garlic cloves, grated

3 tablespoons balsamic vinegar

2 tablespoons fresh lemon juice

1 cup pitted kalamata olives

1 teaspoon red chili flakes, or to taste

Fresh herbs, such as basil, cilantro, and arugula

2 cups cooked orzo (see Note)

1 cup cubed fresh mozzarella cheese

2 tablespoons grated Parmesan cheese

NOTE Substitute quinoa for the orzo to make the dish gluten-free.

Ratatouille is a French dish, and like the niçoise salad that originated in Nice, it is often a stew, but can also be baked or sautéed. It commonly includes tomatoes, zucchini, garlic, eggplant, and leafy greens.

I must admit that I am a sucker for stuffing food into food, a.k.a. edible food bowls. Plus this ratatouille is great for a beach picnic or boat excursion—boats on boats! There is less waste and less trash with edible food bowls—just wrap the boat in parchment paper, and out you go. These boats can be eaten warm or at room temperature.

Do you need to salt your eggplant before sautéing it to draw out moisture and bitterness, as some recipes state? Do you need to peel the skin off the eggplant? I am going to disagree with both of these steps. Keep it simple—it'll be just as delicious.

Preheat the oven to 375°F.

Slice the eggplants in half lengthwise. We are going to score out the center of each eggplant half to create a "boat": Take a small sharp knife and carve around the edge of the eggplant, leaving a ¼-inch thick "wall" (no need to be exact). Now slice down the center, being careful to not pierce through the skin on the bottom. You can cut a few times crosswise as well, to make it easier to remove the interior. Use a spoon to scoop out the flesh. Chop the cut-out center of the eggplant into a medium dice.

(RECIPE CONTINUES)

NOTE The eggplant boats can be made up to 2 days in advance.

TIP Can you skip the "boat" part of this recipe? Yes, you can. In that case, 1 eggplant will be enough, as you will use all of the eggplant for the ratatouille.

In a large skillet set over medium heat, warm a little oil. Place 2 hollowed-out eggplant halves, cut-side-down in the skillet, and sauté until the edges begin to brown, about 3 minutes. Flip them over and cook for 2 more minutes. (The eggplant shell needs to stay a little undercooked or it will fall apart once you bake it stuffed.)

Set the sautéed eggplant halves aside on a sheet pan and repeat with the remaining halves. Set them aside.

In the same skillet, sauté the chopped eggplant pieces in a little oil, tossing them a few times, until they are browned and soft, 3 to 5 minutes. Transfer them to a medium bowl. Sauté the remaining ingredients, one by one, the same way: zucchini, bell pepper, red onion, cherry tomatoes.

Toss all these vegetables with the sautéed eggplant pieces. Season the mixture with salt to taste and add the garlic, balsamic vinegar, and lemon juice. Stir in the kalamata olives. Toss with the red chili flakes and the herbs. Add the cooked orzo and cubed mozzarella cheese.

Stuff the mixture into the eggplant shells, and sprinkle the tops with the Parmesan cheese. Heat the boats in the oven for 20 to 30 minutes, until the stuffing is heated through and the mozzarella is beginning to melt.

CHOPPED LOBSTER SALAD

SERVES 2

2 small (6-ounce) raw lobster tails

Yuzu Dressing (recipe follows)

2 cups chopped romaine lettuce

1 cup chopped radicchio

Segments from ½ orange, seeded and diced

Segments from ½ grapefruit, seeded and diced

1 cup halved cherry tomatoes

¼ cup green olives, pitted

½ cup thinly sliced red onion

6 scallops (see Note)

Salt and pepper to taste

Olive oil

NOTE How to choose your scallops? Sea scallops are the premium choice, but bay scallops are easier to find—smaller but just as sweet. Scallops are often treated with phosphate chemicals which make them look shiny and fresh under the lights at the fish counter, but that extra weight makes them more costly while also diluting their flavor. The extra moisture also makes it more difficult to get a proper sear. Look for "dry packed" scallops, which have not been treated with chemicals or filled with water.

One day a general inquiry showed up in our email, asking if we would like to open a restaurant in Japan. We assumed it was spam of some sort, but before I knew it, I was on a plane to Tokyo. I got a whirlwind thirty-six-hour tour of Japan, I hiked halfway up Mount Fuyu with a guide who wore a suit, I took a bath in a traditional wooden tub, I ate more than I ever had before, and before I could say *"Arigatō,"* Malibu Farm Zushi Marina was a go. This recipe is from our home by the marina of Sagami Bay.

This restaurant was scheduled to open during the height of the coronavirus pandemic, which of course meant we were not able to travel there for the training or opening celebrations, but we can still enjoy a dish from our team across the ocean.

In a medium pan containing enough water to cover the lobster tails, simmer the tails for 5 to 8 minutes, until they are just cooked through and translucent inside. Drain, and then allow the lobster tails to cool for 10 minutes, or until they are cool enough to handle. With a sharp knife or kitchen shears, cut through the lobster shell lengthwise. Peel off the shell, cut the lobster meat into large pieces, and place the pieces in a small bowl. Stir 1 tablespoon of Yuzu Dressing into the lobster to marinate.

Combine all the salad ingredients (romaine, radicchio, diced orange, diced grapefruit, cherry tomatoes, green olives, and red onion) in a medium bowl.

(RECIPE CONTINUES)

TIP To cook whole lobsters in a butter bath, see my first book, *Malibu Farm Cookbook*, page 180.

To prep the scallops, remove the side muscle, rinse the scallops with cold water, and pat dry, dry, very dry. The scallops will not sear if they are more than slightly moist. Season them lightly with salt and pepper.

Heat a few tablespoons of oil in a large skillet over high heat until it begins to smoke, and add the scallops without crowding the skillet. Sear the scallops for 1½ minutes on each side until golden brown. Let them rest for a couple of minutes off the heat, and then toss the scallops, lobster pieces, and remaining Yuzu Dressing with the salad.

NOTE An opened yuzu juice bottle will last about 4 weeks in the fridge; if you will not use it up in that time frame, freeze the leftover juice in ice cube trays to use later in dressings, aioli, and cocktails.

YUZU DRESSING

MAKES 1 CUP

2 tablespoons fresh lemon juice
¼ cup yuzu juice (half of standard 12-gram bottle)
1 tablespoon Dijon mustard
1 tablespoon soy sauce
A pinch of salt
1 garlic clove, grated
1 teaspoon grated fresh ginger (see Note, page 223)
1 tablespoon honey or agave nectar
⅓ cup cup olive or vegetable oil

In a small bowl, combine the lemon juice and yuzu juice with the mustard, soy sauce, salt, garlic, ginger, honey, and olive oil. Whisk to blend. The dressing will keep for 3 to 5 days in the fridge.

LOBSTER LOUISA ROLLS

SERVES 4

2 pounds lobster meat: claws, tail, and knuckle pieces, cooked (see Note), or bay shrimp, cooked

1 celery stalk, sliced thin

¼ cup thinly sliced fennel

1 teaspoon paprika

1 teaspoon cayenne pepper

⅓ cup chopped fresh herbs (such as parsley, dill, and chives)

¼ cup fresh lemon juice

Juice from 1 lime

½ cup lemon aioli (see page 219) or mayonnaise, purchased or homemade (see page 218)

Salt to taste

4 brioche hot dog buns

4 hard-boiled eggs, sliced thin

½ hothouse cucumber, sliced thin

4 leaves Bibb lettuce or arugula

NOTE Lobsters can be very pricey, so unless you want to splurge, go ahead and use cooked mixed lobster meat (often found frozen). It's usually available in 2-pound bags; defrost it before using. To cook fresh lobster or lobster tails, see Chopped Lobster Salad, page 123.

There are plenty of California spiny lobsters off our coast from fall to spring, and you often find the Malibu beaches littered with their shells, but you never find local lobsters at the grocery store. Apparently all (or most) California lobsters are shipped to China, and most of the lobsters we eat in California come from Maine. Go figure. If you are a Californian and want fresh local lobsters, you've got to put on your wetsuit and catch them yourself, or track down a specialty shop that offers them in season (which begins around October 1). Otherwise, it's East Coast lobsters that we're tossing with the works and stuffing in soft rolls. Since lobster rolls are reminiscent of Swedish bay shrimp sandwiches, you can substitute bay shrimp—a much more affordable and easily available alternative—for the lobster.

In a medium bowl, toss the lobster or bay shrimp with the celery, fennel, paprika, cayenne, herbs, lemon juice, lime juice, and lemon aioli. Season to taste with salt. The salad can be made 1 day in advance and refrigerated.

To assemble, toast your brioche hot dog buns. Fill them with the sliced eggs, cucumber, and the lettuce or arugula, and top with the lobster salad.

LOBSTER LOUISA ROLLS

RAW ARTICHOKE SALAD (page 194)

CANDIED NUTS AND SEEDS

NOTE *Save the seeds!* Yes, you can save the seeds from your pumpkins and your squashes to plant them or to eat them. First rinse the seeds and set them on a sheet pan to dry. Space them out so they do not stick together. Place the pan in a cool dark spot and let the seeds dry, turning them every couple of days. Once the seeds are dry, you can store them, plant them, or roast and eat them.

Candied nuts and seeds make a great addition to salads and vegetables. There are many easy ways to make them. Here are my three favorite ways. We use candy sesame seeds with cheese and fruit, but try fennel, cumin, or mustard seeds for crunchy sweet and spicy additions.

AGAVE OR HONEY SEEDS OR NUTS

1 cup raw or roasted pepitas (pumpkin seeds), sunflower seeds, or any seeds or nuts

3 tablespoons agave nectar or honey

Salt to taste

Cayenne pepper to taste (optional)

2 tablespoons powdered sugar (optional)

In a dry skillet over medium heat, sauté the pepitas, sunflower seeds, or any seeds or nuts with the agave or honey until they just begin to brown. Transfer the seeds or nuts to a baking sheet and let them cool. Sprinkle with salt to taste and a little cayenne pepper if you like. Once the seeds or nuts have cooled, you can chop them up or leave them whole.

You can do this with any seeds or nuts. Because they are sautéed in agave or honey, they will always be slightly *tacky* as in sticky, not *tacky* as in lack of style. This treat is always in fashion. You can dust the nuts in powdered sugar after cooking to make them less sticky.

(RECIPE CONTINUES)

TIPS Try black sesame seeds; they look cool.

Using regular sugar, as opposed to agave or honey, makes the seeds dry, not sticky.

If you like monk fruit sweetener, you can substitute it for the sugar, but add the seeds to the skillet first and then add the sweetener. As soon as the sweetener is melted, it is done.

CANDIED SEEDS

¼ cup white or brown sugar (see Tips)

¾ cup roasted seeds (sesame seeds, poppy seeds, flaxseeds, hemp seeds, fennel seeds, mustard seeds)

Salt to taste

In a small dry skillet over low heat, melt the sugar without stirring it, 2 to 3 minutes. As soon as the sugar has turned into melted caramel, quickly stir in the seeds until combined. (You want more seeds than sugar. Too much sugar will make the seeds too hard, so add more seeds if needed.) Pour the seeds onto a sheet pan, season them with salt, and allow them to dry. Chop as needed. (The melted sugar will be extremely hot, so be careful not to touch it or you may burn your fingers!)

Candied seeds will last for several weeks in a covered container at room temperature.

CRISPY WALNUTS OR PECANS

I love these. They are the best of the best when it comes to candied nuts—a little more work than the others but so worth it. You will not be disappointed.

2 cups raw walnuts or pecans

1 cup vegetable oil

¾ cup confectioners' sugar

Salt to taste

Cayenne pepper to taste

Fill a small pan with enough water to cover the walnuts or pecans, bring it to a boil, and then add the nuts and boil for 5 minutes. Drain, and allow the nuts to dry for 5 minutes. (If you do not boil the nuts, the confectioners' sugar will not adhere properly to them, but you don't want the nuts to be so wet that the confectioners' sugar melts as soon as it is tossed with the nuts. We are looking for the Goldilocks moment when they are just right.)

While the nuts are drying, heat the vegetable oil in a small pan over medium heat. Once the nuts are almost dry, but not fully dry, toss them with the confectioners' sugar so that it coats the nuts. If the confectioners' sugar melts at once, the nuts are still too wet, so wait for a few more minutes. Fry the coated nuts in the hot oil, in three or four batches. Do not crowd the skillet with too many nuts at a time. Once the coated nuts are browned, 2 to 3 minutes per batch, use a slotted spoon and transfer them to a sheet pan. Continue to fry in batches until all the nuts are done.

Season the fried nuts with salt and cayenne pepper to taste. Allow the nuts to cool before using them. These nuts will last for several weeks in the pantry—except they won't, because you will finish them lickety-split.

AFTERNOON FIKA

Swedish **FIKA** is the taking of coffee or tea with snacks that can be **SWEET OR SAVORY.** It is a favorite pastime of all Swedes, myself included. Fika is a **STATE OF MIND**, a ritual, and a routine.

I **LOVE** my fika, I **CRAVE** my fika. I fika each and every day around 3 p.m., just as the madness of the lunch rush is subsiding, or when I realize I am **HUNGRY AGAIN.** Depending on the weather and the time of year, my fika might include ice cream or a slice of cake. It could be green tea or chai tea. I have an **AFTERNOON CRAVING** for sweets that is hard to resist, but if I need more energy to make it through the rest of the day, I will eat a **HEALTHY SNACK**, such as hummus, raw crunchy veggies, or cheese as part of my fika.

It doesn't really matter what you eat for your fika—**SWEET OR SAVORY** or both. Nor does it matter when you eat it—morning, afternoon, or night—because it is not about what you eat or when, it is about **HOW YOU FEEL.** To really fika like a Viking, you make fika specially for someone or someone special makes it for you.

My mother loved fika, and when I think of her, I think of fika, and when I fika I think of her. Sometimes I can barely remember a time when I had a mother, it seems so long ago. Other times it seems like just yesterday that she was here. She loved the **SUN**, she loved the **BEACH** and swimming in the **OCEAN**, she loved riding her bicycle everywhere, but most of all **SHE LOVED FIKA.** I think you will, too.

VEGAN CASHEW COCONUT CHERRY ICE CREAM

SWEET CORN ICE CREAM (page 139)

STRAWBERRY-TOPS SORBET (page 138)

VEGAN CASHEW COCONUT CHERRY ICE CREAM

SERVES 4

1½ cups vegan vanilla cashew yogurt (Forager is my favorite vegan yogurt brand)

1 cup coconut milk

¾ cup maple syrup or syrup from the cherries

1 cup dark sweet cherries in heavy syrup (see Tips), drained

2 tablespoons sliced fresh arugula or basil (see Note)

NOTE Could you skip the arugula or basil in this ice cream? Yes, but why? The fresh herbal taste is a lovely counterpoint to the sweet richness of this dessert.

Also known as the Triple C, which is how I named my kids—Celia, Casper, and Caden. Love the kids, love this ice cream, which I can eat all day every day—not too sweet, just right. I've estimated that this recipe serves four, but what is a serving size of ice cream? A tablespoon or a cup? A little or a lot?

In a medium bowl, combine the yogurt, coconut milk, maple syrup, cherries, and arugula or basil.

If you have an ice cream maker, great: churn according to the manufacturer's instructions.

If you do not have an ice cream maker (who does?!), pour the base into a baking dish, place it in the freezer, and stir occasionally, about every hour or so, until it is set, about 6 hours. This ice cream will not be as smooth as an ice cream that has been churned, but it is still a sweet treat.

You can also pour the base into ice-pop molds.

TIPS Oregon Specialty Fruit is my favorite of the readily available brands of dark sweet cherries in syrup. You can also make your own by substituting sweet pitted cherries for the cranberries in the simple syrup berry recipe on page 283.

Use leftover syrup from the drained berries on pancakes, or as a substitute for maple syrup or agave in smoothies, or in salad dressings, such as burrata fruit salad (see my first book, *Malibu Farm Cookbook*, page 132), or as a replacement for the sugar in Strawberry-Tops Sorbet (page 138).

STRAWBERRY-TOPS SORBET

SERVES 4

1 cup white or brown sugar

3 cups fresh strawberries with green tops on

¼ cup fresh lemon juice

TIP Substitute your favorite fruit or berries in this recipe. The standard fruit-to-sugar range, depending on the sweetness of the fruit, is 3 to 5 cups fruit to 1 cup sugar. Too little sugar makes the sorbet freeze too hard. Adding a small shot of alcohol (1 to 2 tablespoons) also prevents the sorbet from freezing too hard; however, add too much liquor and a strawberry daiquiri it is, which is not necessarily a bad thing.

My younger son, Caden, is responsible for Swedish pancakes making it to the cafe menu, and they're now one of our top sellers (see my first book, *Malibu Farm Cookbook,* page 37). He also always eats the tops of strawberries (and the skin of kiwi fruits!), which made me include the tops in many recipes. Did you not know that you can eat the tops of strawberries? Of course you can. So why are we taking them off and discarding them? I made this sorbet for him first, but then it found its way onto the menu. Caden works as a host on the pier, and he eats this almost every day.

This is the simplest, most delicious sorbet. We will waste nothing; we will eat it all.

In a small skillet, combine the sugar with ½ cup of water and heat it over low heat until the sugar is dissolved, about 2 minutes. Transfer the sugar syrup to a blender and add the strawberries and lemon juice. Blend until smooth.

If you have an ice cream maker, great: churn according to the manufacturer's instructions.

If you do not have an ice cream maker, pour the base into a baking dish, place it in the freezer, and stir it occasionally, about every hour or so, until it is set, about 6 hours. This ice cream will not be as smooth as ice cream that has been churned, but it is still a sweet treat.

You can also pour the base into ice-pop molds.

SWEET CORN ICE CREAM

SERVES 6

4 ears fresh corn

4 cups heavy cream

1 (14-ounce) can sweetened condensed milk

Pinch of cayenne pepper

Pinch of ground chipotle pepper

2 tablespoons thinly sliced fresh basil

Summer corn is a sweet treat in our salads, in our tacos, in our paninis, and also in our ice cream. *Yes,* in our ice cream. Try it!

Cut the corn kernels off the cobs and set them aside (don't toss out the cobs just yet).

Pour the heavy cream into a large skillet, add the corn cobs, and simmer gently over low heat for 10 minutes. Do not bring to a full boil, as the cream is likely to boil over and make a mess on your stove.

Remove and discard the cobs. Transfer the cream to a large bowl and let it cool to room temperature. Then stir the corn kernels, sweetened condensed milk, cayenne pepper, and chipotle pepper into the cooled cream. Transfer the mixture to a blender or food processor, and process until the corn kernels are pulverized. For a smoother texture, strain the mixture.

Gently stir in the sliced basil leaves.

If you have an ice cream maker, great: churn according to the manufacturer's instructions.

If you do not have an ice cream maker, pour the base into a baking dish, place it in the freezer, and stir occasionally, about every hour or so, until set, about 6 hours. This ice cream will not be as smooth as ice cream that has been churned, but it is still a sweet treat.

You can also pour the base into ice-pop molds.

CAFFE LATTE ICE CREAM

SERVES 6

½ cup sugar

1 cup brewed espresso or strong coffee, chilled

1 (12-ounce) can evaporated milk

1 (14-ounce) can sweetened condensed milk

2 cups heavy cream

1 teaspoon vanilla extract

1 teaspoon salt

¼ cup ground espresso beans

I love caffe latte and I love ice cream, so what is better than caffe latte ice cream? Don't like coffee? Use your favorite strongly brewed tea: chai, matcha, chamomile, or Earl Grey!

In a blender, combine the sugar, brewed coffee, evaporated milk, condensed milk, cream, vanilla, and salt. Process until smooth. (You can also whisk the ingredients together in a large bowl.) Taste for deliciousness.

If you have an ice cream maker, great: churn according to the manufacturer's instructions. Top each serving of the ice cream with 2 teaspoons of the ground espresso.

If you do not have an ice cream maker, pour the base into a baking dish, place it in the freezer, and stir occasionally, about every hour or so, until set, about 6 hours. Once it is set, sprinkle the top with the ground espresso beans. This ice cream will not be as smooth as ice cream that has been churned, but it is still a sweet treat.

You can also pour the base into ice-pop molds. In which case, when you take them out of the molds, dip the top of one side of the ice pops into the ground espresso.

VERY BERRY MERINGUE

SERVES 6 TO 8

FOR THE MERINGUE

Vegetable oil

4 egg whites (see Tip)

¾ cup granulated sugar

FOR THE TOPPING

1 cup sliced skin-on almonds, 1 cup sprinkles, or 2 cups Froot Loops

FOR THE FILLING

2 cups heavy cream

2 tablespoons granulated or confectioners' sugar

Fresh berries, bananas, or other fruit, chopped or sliced (about 3 cups)

FOR THE GARNISH

Additional fruits, fresh herbs or arugula, and confectioners' sugar

TIP You used 4 egg whites for the meringue. What to do with the yolks? Saffron Lemon Crème Brûlée (page 145) or Lemon Saffron Pasta Farm onara (page 85) are good options.

A spectacular showpiece for your table, this gluten-free treat is one of my favorites, and you can whip it up quickly. Make it fancy with lots of berries and other fruits, or make it fun by swapping the almond topping for sprinkles or Froot Loops (be mindful, though, that they are not gluten-free). For the center filling, use whipped cream and chocolate, or jam, peanut butter, and bananas—anything you like. More good news: the dessert can be made a day ahead.

Preheat the oven to 375°F.

Line a standard half-size sheet pan with parchment paper, and oil the parchment well.

In a large clean bowl, use a handheld or standing mixer to whip the egg whites until medium peaks form. Then slowly pour in the sugar, whipping all the while, until it is incorporated. It is important to keep the peaks soft and fluffy. Do not whip the mixture to the point that it becomes stiff. The end result of our meringue will be soft. It is better to under-whip than to over-whip.

Spread the whipped meringue mixture on the oiled parchment paper, covering about three-quarters of the sheet pan and leaving at least a 2-inch border of paper on all sides. The mixture should be at least 1 inch thick and does not need to be smooth. Scatter your selected topping over the mixture: almonds, sprinkles, or Froot Loops.

(RECIPE CONTINUES)

Place the sheet pan in the oven and bake the meringue until the top is lightly browned and springs back when you touch it but the meringue is still soft, about 20 minutes. Let it cool for about 5 minutes.

This next step is going to sound more complicated than it is. Just be careful not to burn yourself on the hot sheet pan. Line a second sheet pan with parchment paper (this one needs to be ungreased), invert it over the baked meringue, and flip the whole thing upside down, so that your meringue ends up on the cold sheet pan with the topping on the bottom.

Now gently peel the parchment paper off the baked underside. Wait 5 or so minutes for the meringue to cool. We want it to still be pliable because we will roll it, but if you spread the whipped cream over it when it is too hot, the whipped cream will melt.

While the meringue is cooling, make the filling by whipping the cream with the sugar in a large mixing bowl until stiff peaks form, 1 to 2 minutes.

Once the meringue is cool enough, turn the sheet pan so the long side is facing you, and spread a nice thick layer of whipped cream over three-quarters of the meringue closest to you, leaving the last 2 inches on the far edge without whipped cream. Over the whipped cream, spread the chopped or sliced berries or other fruits. Then roll up the meringue like a jelly roll, starting with the long side nearest you and ending with the seam facing down. The meringue is soft, so use the parchment paper to protect the meringue as you roll it. At this point, you can put the meringue, rolled in the parchment, in the fridge overnight.

Before serving, garnish the meringue with additional fruits or berries, something green, such as herbs or—yes, of course—arugula, and a dusting of confectioners' sugar.

SAFFRON LEMON CRÈME BRÛLÉE

SERVES 4

- ½ cup sugar, plus more for caramelizing the top
- 2 teaspoons lemon zest
- 4 egg yolks (save the egg whites to make meringue, page 143)
- A few strands of saffron
- 2 tablespoons hot water
- 2½ cups heavy cream
- 1 teaspoon vanilla extract

TIP Love the combo of saffron and lemon? Make Lemon Saffron Pasta Farm-onara (page 85). Or make delicious saffron ice cream with lemon (see my first book, the *Malibu Farm Cookbook*, page 280).

The Very Berry Meringue on page 143 left you with four egg yolks. To throw them out would be a crime against Mother Nature; we try to use all the bits and pieces we have. So use them in this saffron-tinted crème brûlée—two showstopping desserts for the price of four eggs. The yolks' color is emphasized by the saffron, and I adore its elusive flavor. What does saffron really taste like? Flowers, honey, or umami? Or perhaps sunshine and history?

I love easy mix-and-pour desserts, with no kneading, no rising, and no need for precision. Simple ingredients—sugar, eggs, and cream—are all we need to make the dessert of our dreams. The most difficult part of the crème brûlée, which isn't particularly difficult, is to brûlée the top. To do it well, you need a kitchen blowtorch. Yes, you can do it under the broiler, but it can be a challenge to do it without burning the sugar or the filling.

If you do not have a torch, do not want to purchase a torch, and do not wish to brûlée under the broiler, no problem: Fill the bottom of the dish or dishes with caramel—made by heating ½ cup of sugar in a dry skillet until melted and deep brown. Let it cool to harden—then add the yolks-and-cream mixture, skip adding the caramelized sugar on the top, and a flan it is. Yeah, yeah, yeah, a fancy baker might disagree about calling this a flan, but here on the farm it will be delicious with the caramel either on the top or on the bottom.

(RECIPE CONTINUES)

NOTE What is a water bath? It is simply a water-filled pan that holds your ramekins while they bake in the oven. It helps ensure even and slow cooking. Use a roasting pan or any shallow pan, and add just enough water to come halfway up the sides of your ramekins.

Preheat the oven to 325°F.

Combine the sugar with the lemon zest in a food processor, and process to make lemon sugar. (You can make the lemon sugar in advance and keep it covered. If it has dried and clumped together by the time you are trying to use it, run it through the processor again so that it is free of lumps.)

Using a handheld mixer or the whisk attachment in a standing mixer, whisk the yolks with the lemon sugar for about 3 minutes, until ribbons form and the yolks turn light in color.

In a small bowl, dissolve the saffron in the hot water until the color is released. Then stir in the heavy cream. Transfer the saffron cream to a small saucepan and heat it gently for a few minutes until the cream is warm but not boiling. With the whisk running, slowly pour the heated cream into the egg mixture until just combined. Do not over-whip, as we do not want too much air in the mixture. Stir in the vanilla. (You can keep this mixture in the fridge for a few days before baking.)

If you are using shallow individual-size ramekins, pour the mixture into them, filling them three-quarters of the way. Place the filled ramekins in a water bath (see Note), and bake them in the oven for about 20 minutes.

For a large, family-style baking dish, pour the mixture into it, place the baking dish in a water bath, and bake for 30 to 40 minutes.

Remove the water bath from the oven, lift the ramekins or baking dish out of it, and chill them for at least 2 hours in the fridge. (This crème brûlée base can be made up to 3 days in advance and kept chilled.)

When you are ready to serve the dessert, sprinkle 1 tablespoon of sugar over the top of each ramekin (or sprinkle approximately 4 tablespoons over a single baking dish). Caramelize the top with a kitchen torch, or very carefully under the broiler, until the sugar is browned and crisp. Serve at once. (Once it is caramelized, the sugar will melt if it is held for an extended time.)

GRANOLA COCONUT CARROT CAKE

SERVES 8

THE GOOD STUFF

3 cups grated carrots (about 3 large carrots)

Zest from 1 orange (about 1 tablespoon)

THE DRY STUFF

2 cups all-purpose flour

1½ cups white or brown sugar

1 teaspoon baking soda

2 teaspoons baking powder

1 teaspoon ground cinnamon

1 teaspoon salt

THE WET STUFF

½ cup olive oil

½ cup canola oil

4 large eggs, beaten

TO FINISH

Coconut Frosting (recipe follows)

Coconut granola or any granola of your choice (purchased or homemade)

TIP In a hurry? Make a sheet cake! Just spread the batter on a greased sheet pan and cut your baking time in half.

We serve our carrot cake with coconut granola on top, so that means it's both breakfast and a dessert contender, right? There is no coconut in the cake itself, only coconut milk in the frosting and coconut in the granola. Buy granola at the store or make your own—there's a recipe in my first book, *Malibu Farm Cookbook,* page 41, that will work great here. Experiment with the cake recipe. Zucchini instead of carrot, yes, yes. Want to switch out all-purpose flour for whole-wheat or gluten-free? Go for it. Add some nuts or raisins? Did you say dates? Ooh, bacon-date carrot cake? Your imagination is your creation.

Preheat the oven to 350°F.

Start by combining the "good stuff" (carrots and orange zest) in a medium bowl. Then stir together the "dry stuff" (flour, sugar, baking soda, baking powder, cinnamon, salt) in a second medium bowl, and whisk together the "wet stuff" (oils, eggs) in a third medium bowl. Yes, that's a lot of bowls, but now three bowls will become one bowl and one cake.

Combine the contents of the wet bowl with the contents of the dry bowl to make the cake batter. Then fold in the "good stuff."

Pour the batter into a greased 10-inch cake pan, a standard loaf pan, or a muffin tin. Bake for about 1 hour if using a cake pan or loaf pan, and about 20 minutes if using a muffin tin. (As a general baking rule, a smaller higher pan like a loaf pan

(RECIPE CONTINUES)

NOTE Almost all cake recipes require that you combine the wet ingredients and the dry ingredients in separate bowls before mixing them together. This is a good practice, and the best way to tackle most baking recipes.

will take longer to bake than a larger shallower baking dish, so adjust the time accordingly.) If the cake starts to brown before the center is cooked, cover the top with foil. The cake is done when the sides begin to pull away, and the top feels springy if you press with your finger.

To serve the cake, cut it into slices, drizzle them with the coconut frosting, and garnish with a handful of your favorite coconut granola. (Or add the frosting and granola to each muffin.)

COCONUT FROSTING

MAKES ABOUT 1 CUP

1 cup confectioners' sugar
¼ cup coconut milk
2 teaspoons vanilla extract

In a small bowl, whisk the confectioners' sugar with the coconut milk and vanilla. For a thinner frosting, add more coconut milk. For a thicker frosting, add more confectioners' sugar. This frosting is thin and will spill over the slices of the cake.

PUMPKIN CHOCOLATE BREAD PUDDING

SERVES 6

¾ cup sugar
6 large eggs
3 cups heavy cream
1 cup canned pumpkin puree
1 teaspoon vanilla extract
5 slices brioche bread, cubed
½ cup chocolate syrup
Tequila Sauce (recipe follows) or whipped cream, for serving

TIP Turn this into French toast the next morning (see page 32).

This is essentially the same recipe as our breakfast Coconut Berry French Toast (page 32). See how much fun you can have making bread puddings! Learn how to make one, and you can make many variations of the same recipe.

Preheat the oven to 375°F.

Pour ½ cup of the sugar into a dry 6-inch or 8-inch cast-iron skillet, and heat it over low heat, without stirring, until it turns into caramel, 2 to 3 minutes. (Stirring could cause it to crystallize, which we do not want.)

Remove the skillet from the heat and set it aside. (It will become your serving dish.) The caramel will harden as it cools.

In a large bowl, whisk together the eggs, cream, pumpkin puree, remaining ¼ cup sugar, and the vanilla. Once the mixture is well combined, stir in the brioche cubes and let the bread soak up the liquid for at least 30 minutes. You can do this the day before and chill in the fridge overnight.

Pour the soaked brioche cubes over the hardened caramel in the skillet. Use all of the liquid. Drizzle with the chocolate syrup. Bake in the oven for about 30 minutes, until the pudding has set. Serve with the Tequila Sauce or whipped cream.

(RECIPE CONTINUES)

TIP Pour this over ice cream, chocolate cake, strawberries, or bananas. Yeah, it goes with pretty much everything.

TEQUILA SAUCE

MAKES 1½ CUPS

So good, so delicious, and so easy to make.

¼ cup maple syrup or agave nectar
1 cup heavy cream or coconut milk
1 shot (1½ ounces) golden tequila

Add the maple syrup or agave nectar to the heavy cream or coconut milk in a small saucepan, and reduce the mixture over low heat until thick and syrupy, 15 to 20 minutes. If you want it to be sweeter, you can add a touch more sweetener or reduce the sauce further.

I like my tequila straight up, so I add 1½ ounces of golden tequila to the sweetened heavy cream or coconut milk. But if you want to burn off the alcohol, pour the tequila into a pan and heat it until it bubbles. Light it on fire with a match or lighter. Always be careful when working with flames! The liquor will catch fire when the flame is within 1 inch. Once the flame is extinguished, the alcohol has burned off. Now you can stir the tequila into the sweetened heavy cream or coconut milk and serve it to the kids. Time to get the party started.

FRESH MINT TEA

SERVES 2

3 sprigs fresh mint

4 cups boiling water

Honey or other sweetener (optional)

Fresh lemon juice (optional)

1 shot ginger juice (optional)

Fika is traditionally had with coffee or tea, so choose your favorite beverage. I love fresh mint tea. The simplest versions of tea are often the best things to give you a moment of peace.

A French press or other clear glass teapot is the most visually stimulating way to steep your mint, but you can also steep it right in your cup or regular teapot. Sweetener and lemon can be added per your taste. Even a shot of fresh ginger juice goes well. Dry mint is not recommended for this.

Place the mint sprigs in a teapot, pour the boiling water over the mint, and let it steep for a few minutes.

If you like, stir in honey or other sweetener, lemon juice, and ginger juice—or some combination of these. Drink. Zen.

STRAWBERRY-TOPS SHAKE

SERVES 1 TO 2

2 cups plain or vanilla yogurt (whole-milk or vegan)

1 frozen banana, chopped

10 frozen strawberries with tops

¾ cup organic whole milk or milk alternative

½ cup honey, maple syrup, or agave nectar, or to taste (optional)

TIP Keep the strawberries' edible tops and blend them into the smoothie. There's no reason to toss the crowns away. Mother Nature grew them and we will eat them.

Summertime, shake time. We use frozen yogurt for our milkshakes because we have a soft-serve machine. I'm going out on a limb here by guessing that you do not have a soft-serve machine at home. Am I right? Use frozen fruit instead. If you are using tart yogurt, you will likely need to sweeten it with honey, but if you are using vanilla yogurt, most are sweet enough that no additional sweetener is needed.

Combine the yogurt, banana, strawberries, milk, and honey or other sweetener in a blender and process until delicious.

MALIBU
FARM
FRESH. ORGANIC. LOCAL.
MALIBU
FARM
FRESH. ORGANIC. LOCAL.

KALE-FORNIA SMOOTHIE

SERVES 1 OR 2

1 cup fresh kale leaves

½ apple, peeled and chopped, or 4 strawberries

½ frozen banana, chopped

3 pitted Medjool dates

6 raw skin-on almonds, walnuts, or pecans

½ cup almond milk, whole milk, or milk alternative

2 tablespoon agave nectar

½ cup ice or water

California is Kale Central. When we first opened the cafe, our local farmer, Larry Thorne, gave us a large donation of apples, and we made apple juice. Which nobody bought. Add kale, said my son Casper, and so we did, and kale apple juice flew off the shelf faster than we could make it. Our Kale-fornia Smoothie and Kale Apple Serrano Hot Sauce (page 61) were soon to follow. Start your day the kale-fornia way with kale, apples, berries, and dates. We use curly kale (curls rule!) for our juices and smoothies, but you choose your favorite kale. Purple kale makes a great color drink.

In a blender, combine the kale, apple, banana, dates, almonds, almond milk, agave, and ice or water. Blend until delicious.

PRETTY IN PINK CHEESECAKE

SERVES 6 TO 8

COOKIE MONSTER CRUST

1½ cups cookie or graham cracker crumbs

6 tablespoons (¾ stick) salted butter (optional), melted

⅓ cup white or brown sugar (optional)

FOR THE CAKE FILLING

1 small raw red beet, peeled and cut into chunks (about ½ cup)

2 (8-ounce) packages cream cheese

1 (14-ounce) can sweetened condensed milk

1 teaspoon vanilla extract

1 teaspoon fresh lemon juice

FOR A NO-BAKE CAKE (OPTIONAL)

1 cup heavy cream whipped with 2 tablespoons confectioners' sugar until stiff

FOR A BAKED CAKE

3 large eggs

TO FINISH

Green Basil Sour Cream Frosting (recipe follows)

Assorted fresh berries or fruit, for garnish

To bake or not to bake?

You decide. You can bake or not bake this cake, according to your mood. Not baking means no cracking, no oven watching, but also a softer cheesecake, almost like a pudding. If you decide to bake, go slow and low to prevent any pesky cracks from forming in the top.

Let's talk about the crust. Why the obsession with graham cracker crusts for cheesecakes? Why those cookies? You can make your crust with any cookie in your pantry. I like to make one with salted caramel cookies, for example. Add sugar depending on the sweetness of your cookie. With a traditional graham cracker crust, you need to add sugar and butter, but if you are using salted caramel cookies or any other sweet, softer cookies, you will not need either.

I recommend using a removable-bottom (springform) pan, because it is impossible to get the cake out otherwise, especially with a no-bake cake. Trust me. I have tried and I have failed. You can use an 8-inch or a 10-inch round pan, or a rectangular pan. The smaller the pan, the higher the baked cake, which means a longer bake time. A large pan means a lower cake, which bakes faster.

You can use any color beet—or you can use carrot or basil—to color your filling and make it happy and bright.

(RECIPE CONTINUES)

First, make the Cookie Monster Crust. The cookies you use will determine how to proceed. I know this is vague, but trust me just a little here, because there are variables. First of all, what cookie you select will determine how many you need. You'll need 1½ cups cookie crumbs for this recipe, so grind up your cookies in a food processor (about 3 to 5 large regular cookies, or 33 graham cracker squares).

Try to squeeze some of the crumbs together with your fingers. If they hold together at all, you do not need to add the melted butter. If they do not hold together, add enough butter to be able to press into a crust.

If you are using sweet cookies that are on the softer side, you will not need to add the sugar.

If your cookies are very dry and not very sweet, such as graham crackers, then add the melted butter and the sugar.

Guess what? You can also bake your crust—or not. I see no reason to bake a crust that has neither melted butter nor sugar added to it. Usually a graham cracker crust with added butter is baked to firm it up, but it is not necessary.

For a no-bake crust, simply press the ground cookies onto the bottom of your cake pan.

For a baked crust, press the ground cookies onto the bottom of your cake pan, place the pan in a preheated 375°F oven, and bake for 8 minutes or until lightly browned. Let the crust cool.

(RECIPE CONTINUES)

NOTE What is a water bath? It is simply a water-filled pan that holds your cake pan while it bakes in the oven. It helps ensure even slow cooking, and prevents cracking in cheesecakes. Use a roasting pan or any shallow pan, and add just enough water to come halfway up the sides of your cake pan. If you are using a removable-bottom cheesecake pan (recommended), first wrap the bottom with foil to prevent water from seeping in.

Once the crust is ready, make the cake filling: Combine the chunks of beet, the cream cheese, and the sweetened condensed milk in a food processor and blend for a few minutes. I like to leave the beets showing in speckles, rather than fully incorporating them into the mixture, but do it however you prefer. Add the vanilla and lemon juice. (We need only a splash of lemon; too much lemon will make the batter too thin.) Now taste the deliciousness and decide if you want to bake or not bake this dessert.

For a No-Bake Cake: The filling will get a little stiffer once it is chilled, but it will always be brightly colored and on the softer side, like a pudding. If you decide to do a no-bake version, you can use the filling as is. Or to give it a little more body, gently fold in the whipped cream. Then pour the filling over the crust, and tap the cake pan against the countertop a few times to settle the filling. Place it in the refrigerator to set for at least 3 hours or overnight. Remove the springform sides and transfer the cake to a serving platter. Spread the Green Basil Sour Cream Frosting over the top and garnish with berries or other fruit.

For a Baked Cake: Preheat the oven to 325°F. Add the eggs to the filling in the food processor (do not add the whipped cream) and incorporate them into the mixture by pulsing a few times. Do not over-blend. Pour the filling over the crust, and smooth the top with a spatula.

To bake the cake, do it slow and low, ideally by setting the cake pan in a water bath (see Note). If it's a removable-bottom cake pan, first wrap the bottom of the pan in a double layer of foil to prevent water from seeping into the crust.

Bake in the oven until the center just wiggles but before it rises in the center, about 1½ hours if you are using an 8-inch pan and 1 hour if you are using a 10-inch pan. An overbaked cake will crack once it cools. Allow the cake to cool in the refrigerator for about 3 hours or overnight, until fully chilled.

Remove the spingform sides and transfer the cake to a serving plate. Spread the Green Basil Sour Cream Frosting over the cake, and decorate it with berries or other fruit.

GREEN BASIL SOUR CREAM FROSTING

MAKES ABOUT 2 CUPS

¼ cup fresh basil leaves
1 cup sour cream or crème fraîche
1 cup confectioners' sugar
1 teaspoon vanilla extract

Combine the basil, sour cream, confectioners' sugar, and vanilla in a food processor and blend until just combined. The frosting will be loose and will spill over the sides of the cake.

DATE ME DESSERT

SERVES 6

1 cup pitted Medjool dates (about 8 dates), chopped fine

1 teaspoon baking soda

½ cup honey or agave syrup

3 tablespoons salted butter

2 large eggs

1 teaspoon vanilla extract

½ cup whole-wheat, gluten-free, or all-purpose flour

1 teaspoon baking powder

1 teaspoon kosher salt

Vegetable or olive oil, for greasing the muffin tin or ramekins

Am I a muffin or a pudding?

It is all in the eye of the beholder. You can eat this goodie like a soft delicious muffin, or you can serve it with tequila sauce (see page 152) or with maple syrup, whipped cream, and caramelized walnuts—and a dessert pudding it is.

Preheat the oven to 375°F.

Put the chopped dates in a small saucepan, add 1 cup of water, and boil until the water is almost evaporated, about 10 minutes. Remove from the heat and stir in the baking soda. Let the mixture cool for a few minutes, and then stir in the honey and butter until combined.

In a medium bowl, whisk together the eggs and vanilla. Add the eggs to the date mixture.

In a medium bowl, sift together the flour, baking powder, and salt. Add the date mixture and stir to combine.

Pour the batter into a greased 6-muffin tin or into greased individual ramekins, and bake until the top springs back when touched, about 30 minutes.

The muffins will be fairly soft. You can cool and eat them as muffins, or serve them warm and garnish them with tequila sauce (see page 152) or maple syrup, whipped cream, and caramelized walnuts (see page 128).

APPLE CRANBERRY CAKE

SERVES 6 TO 8

THE GOOD STUFF

5 apples or pears (your favorite variety), peeled, cored, and chopped

3 tablespoons white or brown sugar

1 tablespoon ground cinnamon

2 cups fresh cranberries (see Tip)

1 cup raw walnuts or pecans

THE DRY STUFF

2¾ cups all-purpose, whole-wheat, or gluten-free flour

1 tablespoon baking powder

1 teaspoon salt

2 cups white or brown sugar

THE WET STUFF

1 cup olive or vegetable oil, or 50/50 blend

¼ cup orange, apple, or cranberry juice

2½ teaspoons vanilla extract

4 large eggs

Vegetable oil or butter, for greasing the pan

FOR SERVING

Whipped cream

Simple syrup cranberries (page 283), optional

I am all about the holidays. I buy pumpkins in July, and I dream of Thanksgiving decor and Christmas trees in August. I shriek in delight when fresh cranberries arrive, and this sweet, tart cake will be just what I crave as soon as Labor Day is over and school starts, because by that time the holidays are essentially here. Use apples or pears, but the cranberries are what make this cake a sweet and tart treat.

Preheat the oven to 375°F.

Start by combining the "good stuff" (the apples, sugar, cinnamon, cranberries, and walnuts) in one large bowl. Then stir together the dry ingredients (flour, baking powder, salt, sugar) in a second medium bowl, and whisk together the wet ingredients (oil, juice, vanilla, eggs) in a third medium bowl. Yes, that's a lot of bowls, but now three bowls will become one bowl and one cake.

Combine the contents of the wet bowl with the contents of the dry bowl to make the cake batter. Then fold in the "good stuff." It is going to seem like a lot of apples, but use them all.

Grease a 9-inch baking pan, and pour the mixture into the pan. Bake in the oven for about 1 hour or until the cake has set.

Serve with whipped cream and garnish with simple syrup cranberries, if using.

TIP Use fresh cranberries only. Frozen ones will make the cake too wet.

ZUCCHINI BREAD

SERVES 8

THE GOOD STUFF

1 cup chopped raw walnuts

1 cup chopped pitted Medjool dates

3 cups grated zucchini (about 3 large zucchinis)

THE DRY STUFF

3 cups whole-wheat, gluten-free, or all-purpose flour

1¾ cups white or brown sugar

1 teaspoon baking soda

½ teaspoon baking powder

1 teaspoon salt

THE WET STUFF

4 large eggs

1 cup olive, or vegetable oil, or 50/50 blend

2 teaspoons vanilla extract

¼ cup juice (green, apple, or orange)

Vegetable oil or butter, for greasing the pan

I love eating a sweet treat with coffee or tea, but ideally something not too sweet. That's why carrot and zucchini breads are my favorites.

Preheat the oven to 325°F.

Start by combining the "good stuff" (walnuts, dates, and zucchini) in a large bowl. Then stir together the dry ingredients (flour, sugar, baking soda, baking powder, salt) in a second medium bowl, and whisk together the wet ingredients (eggs, oil, vanilla, juice) in a third medium bowl. Yes, that's a lot of bowls, but now three bowls will become one bowl and one cake.

Combine the contents of the wet bowl with the contents of the dry bowl to make the cake batter. Then fold in the "good stuff."

Grease a 9 x 5-inch loaf pan, and pour the mixture into the pan. Bake for about 1 hour or until the cake is set.

SUNSET

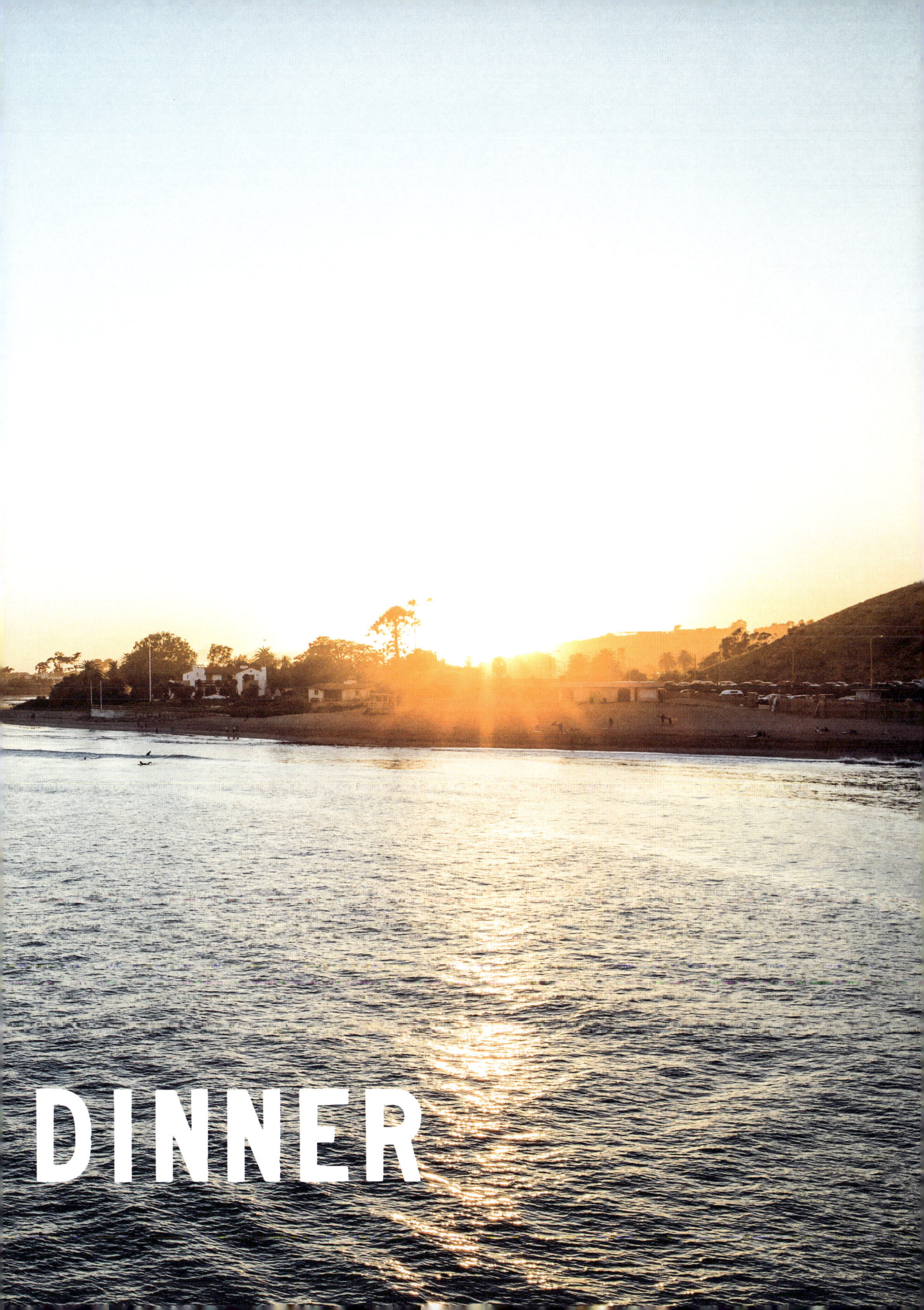

DINNER

The **SUNSET STRIP** (a 1½-mile stretch of Sunset Boulevard) is known worldwide as *the* place to **WALK AND SHOP**, a place that you must see and a place where you must be, and often in Los Angeles the Sunset Strip becomes synonymous with the **SUNSET**.

But there is a different kind of sunset, one **ACCESSIBLE TO ALL**, anywhere you are, no matter who you are or where you are. The **MAGIC OF THE SUNSET** is there for all of us to **LOVE** and to **CHERISH**. When the sun sets, it is the time to **REMEMBER** old friends and make new ones.

The sunset reminds us all to **GATHER** at the table, to take stock of our day and our paths, of goals accomplished and **DREAMS** yet to be fulfilled. It is a time for us to **INVITE** the old and the young, to **RECONNECT** with the past and connect with the future. When the sun sets, set the table, set the longest table you can for as long as you can.

How long a table will we set? How many guests will we invite? Only a lack of **IMAGINATION** can limit this table. It reaches across the **OCEAN** and around the **WORLD**, touching **HEARTS AND SOULS**, turning strangers into **FRIENDS**. No matter where you go, you will find that we all want the same things: seats at the table, our voices heard, and the **FREEDOM** to be who we are.

We will set a table and set aside our differences. We will serve up **INCLUSION**, not division. At the table of our **DREAMS**, there are seats for vegans, vegetarians, and traditional eaters, and together we step out on the path of the **FUTURE** with more vegetables and greens. Tonight there is **NO JUDGMENT**. Everyone is **WELCOME**. Only together can we make **CHANGE**.

NO FISHING AREA

CARROT SOUP

WITH ROASTED TOMATO COULIS

SERVES 4

1 tablespoon salted butter

1 tablespoon olive oil

1 small yellow onion, diced

4 large carrots, peeled and chopped (about 4 cups)

Salt and pepper to taste

4 cups chicken or vegetable broth, or more if needed

1 cup fresh orange juice

Roasted Tomato Coulis (recipe follows), for garnish (optional)

Sour cream or yogurt, agave pepitas (see page 129), or fresh herbs, for garnish (optional)

Sweet and spicy makes for a great winter soup. Can you use sweet potatoes or butternut squash instead of carrots? Yes, you can. And the roasted tomato coulis is a delicious sauce that you can serve with fish, chicken, grilled portobello mushrooms, or steak.

Heat the butter and olive oil in a skillet over medium heat, and sauté the diced onion for about 5 minutes, until translucent. Stir in the carrots and sauté for an additional 5 minutes, being careful not to burn the onions. Season with salt and pepper. Cover the vegetables with the broth, and simmer for about 15 minutes, until the carrots are soft.

Puree the mixture using an immersion blender, or transfer it to a blender and process until smooth. Stir in the orange juice, and thin the soup with additional broth or water until the desired consistency is reached.

Serve as is, or garnish each bowl of soup with a dollop of Roasted Tomato Coulis, or a drizzle of sour cream or yogurt, or a sprinkling of agave pepitas or fresh herbs—or choose all the garnishes.

(RECIPE CONTINUES)

NOTE For additional uses for adobo sauce and canned chipotle chiles, see Note, page 227. Use only the adobo sauce for a less spicy coulis.

ROASTED TOMATO COULIS

MAKES 1 CUP

2 Roma tomatoes, broiled until charred black

1 tablespoon balsamic vinegar

1 teaspoon (or to taste) adobo sauce from canned chipotle chiles in adobo sauce

Dash of sugar

½ teaspoon Worcestershire sauce

Salt and pepper to taste

Combine the tomatoes, vinegar, adobo sauce, sugar, and Worcestershire sauce in a food processor. Whirl, blend, whirl, and add salt and pepper to taste. Done.

THE BIG APPLE SALAD

WITH BRUSSELS SPROUTS

SERVES 4

Olive oil

16 medium Brussels sprouts, halved

Salt to taste

2 red or green apples

Mustard Maple Dressing (recipe follows)

1 bunch black kale (a.k.a. dinosaur kale or Lacinato kale; about 4 cups), chopped

1 cup fresh arugula

2 tablespoons candied sunflower seeds (see page 129), for garnish

I arrived in New York City almost forty years ago, and here I am returning to the Big Apple and opening a restaurant. A modern-day Cinderella story, except with Brussels sprouts, kale, and arugula salad instead of a prince. In fall 2019 we opened our doors to the Big Apple. We've gone from a humble pop-up at the end of the Malibu Pier to opening at Pier 17 in the Seaport District in the Big Apple, New York City.

As soon as the New York City deal was signed, sealed, and delivered, I started obsessing about a Big Apple salad. It took me as long as the construction of the location to finalize this recipe. I wanted it to be apple-delicious but not too sweet. I wanted it to be filling and healthy to eat. The result: this salad cannot be beat. I am totally enamored with this workhorse of a salad, which you can actually toss with dressing and eat the next day.

Preheat the oven to 400°F.

Lightly oil a sheet pan and place the Brussels sprouts, cut-side down, on it. Drizzle the Brussels sprouts with a small amount of oil. Roast the Brussels sprouts in the oven until the cut side starts to brown but before the sprouts get too soft, about 10 minutes. Sprinkle with salt.

(RECIPE CONTINUES)

While the sprouts are roasting, cut the apples into sections (no need to peel them) and then into slices. In a large bowl, toss the apple slices with a small amount of Mustard Maple Dressing to prevent them from turning brown.

Massage the kale lightly with some Mustard Maple Dressing until the leaves become glossy. Then add the kale, arugula, and Brussels sprouts to the apples, and toss.

Garnish the salad with the candied sunflower seeds.

MUSTARD MAPLE DRESSING

MAKES ¾ CUP

2 tablespoons whole-grain mustard

2 tablespoons maple syrup

6 tablespoons apple cider vinegar (or fresh lemon juice)

¼ cup olive oil

1 garlic clove, grated

Salt to taste

In a small bowl, whisk together the mustard, maple syrup, apple cider vinegar, olive oil, and garlic. Add salt to taste. This dressing can be made up to 3 days in advance and stored in the refrigerator.

SPAGHETTI SQUASH LASAGNA

SERVES 4

2 6- to 8-inch spaghetti squashes

Salt to taste

Juice from 1 lemon

1 tablespoon olive oil

1 garlic clove, grated

4 cups tomato sauce, purchased or homemade

4 cups Classic Creamy Béchamel (recipe follows)

2 cups chopped fresh mozzarella cheese

2 cups shredded three-cheese blend (Monterey Jack, Colby, and Cheddar cheeses)

TIP You can make many variations of spaghetti squash lasagna—for example, with pesto, ricotta cheese, and kale. Also, you can add cooked ground turkey, chicken, or beef to the lasagna when you assemble the layers.

This isn't a real lasagna, as there is no pasta in sight. At Malibu Farm, pizzas aren't pizzas, and falafel isn't falafel. They may remind us of the original dish, and they pay homage to it, but they are an interpretation of the classic dish. I love the classics as much as anyone, and sometimes the traditional way is the only way, but our Malibu way makes room to explore a classic recipe.

This lasagna recipe is a top-selling entrée for us, but every now and then a guest will tell us it is not a "real" lasagna. Okay—but what is the definition of *real?* This lasagna contains almost all the traditional ingredients. The only swap is the squash strands for the pasta sheets.

Preheat the oven to 400°F.

Cutting spaghetti squash can be difficult, as the squash is very hard. Please do not cut yourself—this is the number one priority. If you do not feel comfortable cutting the squash in half when it is raw, then place both squashes in a large pot, add enough water to cover them, and boil them for 30 minutes, or until just soft when pierced. Do not overcook them. Allow the squashes to cool and then cut them in half lengthwise.

If you are able to cut the squashes raw, cut off the ends of each squash first, slicing off just about ½ inch. Once the ends are cut off, place the squash upright, resting on a cut end, which will give the squash some stability while you cut it.

(RECIPE CONTINUES)

VEGAN OPTION In place of the béchamel sauce, use vegan sour cream (page 109) thinned with ¼ cup oatmilk or any alternative milk. Instead of cheese, use vegan ricotta, made by roughly mashing together 1 cup firm tofu, 2 tablespoons nutritional yeast, 1 grated garlic clove, and a splash of lemon juice.

Now carefully slice the squash down the center so you have two halves of the squash. *Phew,* you did it! It will get easier each time. Place the squash halves, cut-side up, on a sheet pan, fill the cavity of each squash half with 1 inch of water, and bake in the oven for 30 minutes or until just soft when pierced.

However you may have cooked your squash, now use a fork to pull out the spaghetti strands and hollow out the shells. We will be using the shells for serving, so don't toss them out. Transfer the strands to a bowl, and season them with salt to taste and the lemon juice, olive oil, and garlic.

Once you have all your lasagna components gathered, you just need to layer them in your squash shells: first the squash strands, then the tomato sauce, béchamel sauce, mozzarella, and three-cheese blend. Repeat the layers, ending with the three-cheese blend on top. (These lasagnas can be made up to 2 days in advance. Just put them in your fridge until you are ready to eat them.)

To serve, bake the lasagnas in the 400°F oven until warm all the way through, about 40 minutes.

NOTE For a gluten-free béchamel, use cornstarch instead of flour by combining 2 tablespoons cornstarch with 3 tablespoons water and whisking the mixture into the milk and cream mixture—no butter or oil needed.

CLASSIC CREAMY BÉCHAMEL

MAKES 4 CUPS

Béchamel? Just a fancy French word for cream sauce. I was taught to always heat milk to make the béchamel, and one day I said, Why? Because some fancy chef told us so? Well, here is a fact about making a classic béchamel: The most difficult step is keeping the sauce smooth. Do you know what makes it lumpy? When it heats and thickens faster and quicker than you can stir it. This means that if you use cold milk, it is so much easier to prevent lumps.

I like to make my bechamel extra creamy by adding heavy cream. And I add spinach because why not? For a lighter sauce, skip the cream and use 4 cups of milk instead.

4 tablespoons salted butter or olive oil
4 tablespoons all-purpose flour
3½ cups cold whole milk
½ cup heavy cream
4 cups fresh baby spinach
Salt to taste

In a small saucepan, melt the butter or olive oil over medium-low heat. Then stir in the flour until you have a smooth paste. Remove the pan from the heat and whisk in the cold milk.

Once the ingredients are thoroughly combined, return the pan to low heat and slowly bring the sauce to a gentle simmer while whisking it constantly. When the sauce is thick enough to coat the back of a spoon, after 5 to 8 minutes, it is done. Stir in the heavy cream and spinach and season to taste with salt.

ORANGE YOU GLAD EGGPLANT

SOY JOY MARMALADE

½ cup orange marmalade

⅓ cup soy sauce

1 garlic clove, grated (optional)

1 tablespoon grated fresh ginger (optional)

1 teaspoon red chili flakes (optional)

EGGPLANT

¼ cup olive oil or an olive vegetable oil blend

1 large eggplant, cubed

Salt to taste

2 tablespoons seasoned rice vinegar (optional)

2 tablespoons chopped fresh herbs, such as basil, parsley, or dill

NOTE To prevent your eggplant from absorbing a lot of oil, place the cubed eggplant in a single layer on a paper towel–lined plate before sautéing and microwave for 5 minutes.

Love eggplant? Try the eggplant orzo ratatouille on page 121.

My home kitchen often resembles the feet of the legendary shoemaker's children—bare, or nearly so. I find myself staring into an almost empty fridge in search of ingredients to make a meal. Sometimes I end up whipping up something embarrassingly simple, but hey, it is true that mixing rice vinegar with soy sauce is delicious and the result goes with practically anything, and the same is true of mixing marmalade with soy sauce. When we think we have nothing, there is always something—in life, in love, and in the fridge. In the very back of the fridge there is an old jar of orange marmalade that has been sitting there for who knows how long, but it is still good, and we will thin it with soy sauce, and out of practically nothing, we have made a sauce that is sticky-sweet and full of joy.

Eggplant is an underappreciated vegetable, but wait, did you know eggplant is not a vegetable? It is a fruit—a berry, in fact. How berry amazing is that? It is part of the nightshade family of flowering plants, which includes tomatoes, chile peppers, potatoes, and capsicums. You can make this dish a nightshade celebration and add bell peppers, chiles, and cherry tomatoes to the dish.

Make the soy joy marmalade: In a large bowl, combine the marmalade with the soy sauce. Stir in the garlic, ginger, and red chili flakes if desired. The sauce will last for one week in the fridge.

(RECIPE CONTINUES)

TIPS Got other flavored marmalades, preserves, or jams sitting in the back of your fridge? Go ahead and try them. Fig jam soy joy would be delicious.

The sauce is great with any vegetable—use it as a dip for crudités. You can also add a splash of rice vinegar and turn it into a glaze for chicken or pork.

And, yes, you can make the lazy person's—or perhaps it is the wise person's—version of orange chicken this way. Don't tell General or Madame Tso.

Heat a large skillet over medium heat and add the oil. Sauté the eggplant cubes until brown and crispy, turning once, about 5 minutes.

Season the eggplant with salt and the rice vinegar, if using. Serve with the Soy Joy Marmalade on the side, or toss to coat, and garnish with herbs. Serve as a side dish or turn it into a vegetarian main with the addition of rice, quinoa, or another grain.

MONSTER SPROUTS

WITH HOT HONEY DIP

SERVES 4

8 very large Brussels sprouts
Olive oil
Salt
Hot Honey Dip (recipe follows)

We have cooked Brussels sprouts many delicious ways through the years—mostly roasted and occasionally sliced thin to eat raw. But sometimes the sprouts in the market aren't medium size. Sometimes they are a giant monster size and we are not sure what to do with them (see page 101 for examples). To prepare these beauties, we pick the leaves off one by one for a special-occasion, bountiful Brussels bouquet of deliciousness.

Preheat the oven to 375°F.

Peel the leaves off the Brussels sprouts, one by one. It will be easy at first and get a little harder as you get closer to the center, where you may need to cut the core down in order to remove the inner leaves. As you work, toss the leaves into a large bowl.

Toss the separated leaves lightly with olive oil, and sprinkle them with salt. Spread the leaves out loosely on a sheet pan. Do not crowd the pan with too many leaves. Depending on the size of your sprouts, you are likely to need more than one sheet pan.

Roast the Brussels sprouts leaves in the oven for 10 minutes, or until they begin to brown and crisp. Toss them a few times while they roast, and check on their progress. How long it takes is going to depend on how many leaves you have in your oven. Do you have a handful or a mountain? A mountain is going to give off a lot of steam and take longer

(RECIPE CONTINUES)

than just a few leaves will, but spreading the leaves out on several sheet pans will allow them to crisp up faster.

Remove the sheet pans from the oven and drizzle the sprouts leaves with some of the Hot Honey Dip. To serve, arrange the leaves on a platter alongside the remaining dip in a small bowl. Eat the roasted leaves with your hands, the way you eat chips.

HOT HONEY DIP

MAKES 1½ CUPS

This spicy sweet sauce brings out the natural sweetness in roasted vegetables and fruit, but it's equally delicious brushed on grilled chicken, drizzled on soft cheese like brie or goat cheese, and spread on biscuits, corn bread, or toast.

1 cup honey or agave nectar

¼ to ½ cup hot sauce, to taste: Sweet and Hot Habanero Sauce (page 60), Kale Apple Serrano Hot Sauce (page 61), Sriracha, or Tabasco sauce

Combine the honey or agave with ¼ cup hot sauce in a small bowl. Taste the dip and add more hot sauce until the desired level of spicy heat is reached.

This dip can be made in advance and kept, covered and refrigerated, for up to 2 weeks.

GRILLED KALE THRILLS

SERVES 4

1 bunch of black kale (a.k.a. dinosaur kale or Lacinato kale), leaves kept whole

Olive oil spray

Salt to taste

Lime Cucumber Yogurt Sauce (page 277; optional)

Pucker Up Tahini Sauce (page 278; optional)

NOTE Any kale will BBQ just right. Try curly, baby, red, purple, or white . . . whatever you prefer.

We have massaged our kale for years and eaten it raw, and we still love our raw kale, but sometimes we just want *everything* to go on the barbecue. Black kale is the black dress, black slacks, and black boots of your kitchen: it goes with everything. And now it shines, grilled on the barbecue.

In a grill pan set over high heat or directly on the barbecue grate, grill the kale leaves, spraying them with olive oil spray every now and then, until they are nice and crispy, about 5 minutes. Season with salt to taste.

Drizzle the grilled kale with Lime Cucumber Yogurt Sauce and Pucker Up Tahini Sauce. You can also snack on them as chips, no sauce needed.

RAW ARTICHOKE SALAD

WITH FENNEL, ARUGULA, AND PARMESAN

SERVES 4

Mustard Lemon Dressing (recipe follows)

1 large artichoke

1 fennel bulb

Salt to taste

4 cups fresh arugula

Shaved Parmesan cheese

1 cup cooked grain, such as quinoa or farro, or lentils (optional)

NOTE A photo of this recipe is next to the lobster roll on page 127.

TIP Love artichokes? Try our grilled artichokes with artichoke aioli on page 217.

Growing artichokes is super easy in California; it's one of the first vegetables to be ready for harvest in the spring. Artichokes are also perennials, so each year they sprout back up and give you more. They are a little tedious to clean, but so worth it. For this recipe, make the Mustard Lemon Dressing first, as you need to slice the raw artichokes directly into the dressing to prevent them from turning brown.

Put the Mustard Lemon Dressing in a large bowl and place it nearby.

For this raw salad, we want only the heart of the artichoke. Remove the sharp outer leaves to reveal the lighter center, or heart. With a spoon, carve out the fuzzy center core. Use a mandoline on the thinnest setting to slice the artichoke heart directly into the Mustard Lemon Dressing. (It will turn brown otherwise.) Toss the slices in the dressing so they are well coated.

Now slice the fennel, also on the mandoline, into the dressing as well. Taste for salt.

You can make this ahead and keep it in the fridge for 2 to 3 days.

To serve, allow the salad to come to room temperature and then toss it with the arugula in a large bowl. Sprinkle with Parmesan cheese, and add the grain or lentils if desired.

MUSTARD LEMON DRESSING

MAKES ¾ CUP

Juice from 2 lemons

1 garlic clove, grated

1 tablespoon whole-grain mustard

1 tablespoon mayonnaise, purchased or homemade (see page 218), or vegan sour cream (see page 109)

¼ cup olive oil

Salt to taste

In a bowl, combine the lemon juice, garlic, whole-grain mustard, mayonnaise or sour cream, and olive oil. Stir well and season to taste with salt.

This dressing can be made in advance and kept, covered and refrigerated, for up to 3 days.

THE STREET CORN WEDGE SALAD

SERVES 4

1 tablespoon salted butter or olive oil

Kernels from 2 ears of corn

1 head iceberg lettuce, cut into 4 wedges

Lime-Cilantro Dressing (recipe follows)

1 cup halved cherry tomatoes

1 tablespoon chopped green onions (scallions)

2 tablespoons chopped fresh cilantro

Cayenne pepper or paprika, for garnish

Bacon bits (see page 45; optional)

Old school, new school, still cool—the classic wedge salad is getting a makeover, and we load it up with sweet corn and drizzle it with Lime-Cilantro Dressing. Because sometimes we want to travel back in time, but we want a fresh take on the salad of our memories.

Heat the butter or oil in a small skillet over high heat, and sear the corn kernels for 3 to 5 minutes, until blistered. Allow the corn to cool down before using it.

Place each lettuce wedge on a plate and drizzle it with dressing. Top with the seared corn, cherry tomatoes, green onions, and cilantro, and sprinkle with a generous dusting of cayenne or paprika. Garnish with bacon bits if using.

LIME-CILANTRO DRESSING

MAKES ¾ CUP

3 tablespoons crème fraîche or sour cream

2 tablespoons mayonnaise, purchased or homemade (see page 218)

¼ cup fresh lime juice (about 2 limes)

1 garlic clove, grated

½ cup crumbled blue cheese, Cotija cheese, or feta cheese

3 tablespoons chopped fresh cilantro

Salt and pepper to taste

In a blender, mix all the ingredients until just combined. This dressing can be made in advance and kept, covered and refrigerated, for up to 3 days.

DILLOVELY ASPARAGUS SALAD

SERVES 4

1 bunch very thick asparagus

½ cup chopped fresh dill

1 thinly sliced watermelon radish or ½ cup thinly sliced red onion (about ½ onion)

Parmesan Lemon Dressing (recipe follows)

4 cups fresh salad greens of your choice

Sometimes they are thin and sometimes they are fat, and both are fabulous. Asparagus, that is. All asparagus shapes and sizes are equally lovely.

Thick asparagus spears are usually peeled, which is the old-school way you find in hotels and Michelin-starred restaurants. I like the skin, and I prefer mine just the way they are. I slice them nice and thin on the mandoline and eat them raw.

Slice the asparagus into thin strips, either crosswise or lengthwise, using a mandoline or sharp knife. (Cutting them lengthwise can be rather dangerous if you are using a mandolin. Even if you slice them crosswise, always be super careful using the mandoline so that you do not cut yourself.)

Place the sliced asparagus in a bowl and add the dill and the slices of watermelon radish or red onion. Pour the Parmesan Lemon Dressing over the mixture, add the salad greens, and toss. This salad goes great with grains such as cooked lentils, quinoa, or farro.

(RECIPE CONTINUES)

TIP Got more large asparagus? Toss lightly with oil and grill them, then drizzle with this dressing and sprinkle with bacon bits and grated hardboiled eggs. Add a healthy grain such as quinoa, farro, or lentils, and dinner is served. This dressing is also great on a bacon, lettuce, and tomato salad.

PARMESAN LEMON DRESSING

MAKES 1 CUP

Juice of 1 lemon (about ¼ cup)

2 tablespoons mayonnaise, purchased or homemade (see page 218)

2 tablespoons grated Parmesan cheese

1 garlic clove, grated

Splash of Worcestershire sauce

¼ cup olive oil

Salt and pepper to taste

In a medium bowl, whisk together the lemon juice, mayonnaise, Parmesan, garlic, and Worcestershire sauce. Then slowly whisk in the oil to emulsify. Season to taste with salt and pepper.

This dressing can be made 3 to 5 days in advance and kept covered in the refrigerator.

THE WHOLE FILLET FISH TACO

SERVES 4

Olive oil

1 whole branzino or 4 skin-on branzino fillets, or fish of your choice (see Note)

Salt

8 to 16 small (4-inch) corn tortillas (2 to 4 per person), warmed

4 cups shredded white or red cabbage

12 radishes, sliced

2 cups shredded jalapeño Jack cheese

Cilantro Crema (recipe follows)

Pico de Gallo (recipe follows)

NOTE If you are using a whole fish, please make sure to have it descaled and cleaned first. Leave the bones in or out, whichever you prefer. Ask the fishmonger to do this for you. Or choose fillets instead, which are ready to cook. A thin fillet like branzino is best with skin on; a thicker fillet can be skinless if you prefer, however skin is tasty and helps keep your fish moist.

Everything is better as a taco or with tacos. Almost all fish tacos come with deep-fried fish, a little cabbage, and salsa, but why fry our treasures from the sea? Let's eat them seared and baked, with lots of delicious sides. That's a dinner to *taco* 'bout.

If you are cooking a whole fish, or a thick piece, preheat the oven to 400°F.

Heat a little oil in a large skillet over high heat. Season the fish lightly with salt and then sauté it in the skillet until the skin is crispy. Flip and cook a few more minutes on the other side. If you are using a thin fillet, you can finish it on the stove. If it is a thicker piece of fish or a whole fish, place it in the oven after searing it in the skillet, and bake for 5 to 20 minutes, depending on the thickness of the fish.

To serve, arrange the fish on a platter and place the tortillas, cabbage, radishes, jalapeño Jack cheese, cilantro crema, and pico de gallo on the side in separate bowls for a build-your-own-taco party.

(RECIPE CONTINUES)

TIP What else can you do with the Cilantro Crema or Pico de Gallo? Pretty much anything. Serve either one—or both—with quesadillas, in a baked potato, with rice and beans, or with grilled shrimp.

CILANTRO CREMA

MAKES 1½ CUPS

1 cup crème fraîche, sour cream, or yogurt

1 cup chopped fresh cilantro

Zest and juice from 1 lime

1 teaspoon salt, or to taste

In a blender or food processor, combine the crème fraîche, cilantro, lime zest and juice, and salt. Blend for a few seconds. Do not over-blend. The crema should be just combined and still speckled with green.

NOTE Serrano chile too hot for you? Use jalepeño instead, as it is 5 to 10 times less spicy than serrano.

PICO DE GALLO

MAKES 1½ CUPS

2 Roma tomatoes, cored and diced

1 small Persian cucumber, diced

¼ cup diced red onion

2 tablespoons chopped fresh cilantro

2 tablespoons chopped fresh mint

1 teaspoon chopped serrano chile pepper (about ½ pepper), or to taste (see Note)

Juice from 1 lime

1 teaspoon salt, or to taste

In a small bowl, combine the tomatoes, cucumber, and red onion with the cilantro, mint, chile pepper, lime juice, and salt. Toss well. You can make the pico 1 day in advance and store in the fridge.

JUNE
SHINE

GRILLED SALMON

WITH MISO TAHINI SAUCE

SERVES 4

4 salmon fillets or fish of your choice

Salt to taste

2 tablespoons olive oil

2 cups shishito chile peppers

Miso Tahini Sauce (recipe follows)

2 tablespoons pickled sushi ginger

1 teaspoon black sesame seeds for garnish (optional)

2 tablespoons fresh herbs for garnish (optional)

I love the simplicity of grilled fish (or meat or chicken) with just the addition of a cold sauce. You can add as much or as little sauce as desired. This miso tahini sauce is multi-use and works well with vegetables and, really, any protein.

Season the fish lightly with salt. In a large cast-iron skillet, with 1 tablespoon of the oil, sear the salmon fillets until brown, about 2 minutes. (If you are using skin-on fillets, sear the skin side first. If you are using skinless fillets, sear the top side first.) Turn to sear the opposite side, or finish in a preheated 400°F oven until done, about 5 more minutes. Alternatively, you can grill or bake your fish. Depending on the thickness of the fillets, the total cook time will be 8 to 10 minutes.

In a medium bowl, toss the shishito peppers with the remaining 1 tablespoon olive oil. Use the same cast-iron skillet on the stove, or alternatively use the grill if that is where you cooked the fish, and char the peppers, turning them once, for 4 minutes or until blistered. Season with salt.

Place your cooked fish on a platter and drizzle the Miso Tahini Sauce over it. Serve with the charred shishito peppers and pickled sushi ginger. Garnish with black sesame seeds and fresh herbs, if using.

(RECIPE CONTINUES)

NOTE Miso is a traditional and beloved Japanese seasoning made by fermenting soybeans, salt, and koji. Tahini is a paste of hulled sesame seeds, popular in the cuisines of the Mideast, Eastern Mediterranean, South Caucasus, and North Africa.

TIP Toasted sesame oil does not last as long as other oils, going rancid rather quickly. Skip it, unless you think you will use it up before a year has passed. What can you do with leftover toasted sesame oil? A minimalist dressing of toasted sesame oil, rice vinegar, grated ginger, and grated garlic can be used as a finish oil for the chicken stir-fry (page 222) or on the Vegan 'Bu Thai Noodles (opposite). Toasted sesame oil has a low smoke point, so it is not good for sautéing on high heat, but you can drizzle it on your Caramel Nuts Popcorn (page 290), sprinkle it on Candied Seeds (page 130), or use it in Poke'viche (page 93).

MISO TAHINI SAUCE

MAKES 1½ CUPS

If you find yourself with extra miso, make miso butter by combining ½ cup butter and ¼ cup miso. Get creative and add garlic and ginger. You can make a super simple and delicious dressing by combining 2 tablespoons miso with the juice from 1 lemon, 6 tablespoons oil, and 1 garlic clove. No salt needed. Pour over steamed vegetables. For a miso-marinated black cod recipe, see my first book, *Malibu Farm Cookbook,* page 171.

¼ cup white miso paste
¼ cup tahini
¼ cup rice vinegar
2 tablespoons agave nectar
1 tablespoon toasted sesame oil (see Tip; optional)
3 tablespoons olive oil
1 garlic clove, grated
1 tablespoon grated fresh ginger
⅓ cup hot water

In a small bowl, combine the miso paste, tahini, vinegar, agave, sesame oil (if using), olive oil, garlic, and ginger. Whisk together until smooth. The sauce will be rather thick. Stirring up to ⅓ cup hot water into the sauce before serving will make it smooth and thin. Store it in the refrigerator.

The sauce will last for 1 week, and you can drizzle it on any vegetable or tofu, or use it to toss the noodles in the Vegan 'Bu Thai Noodles (opposite page).

VEGAN 'BU THAI NOODLES

SERVES 4

1 (8-ounce) package black rice noodles, or any noodles of your choice

2 tablespoons olive oil

1 cup Miso Tahini Sauce (opposite)

7 ounces tofu (about ½ standard packet)

1 cup shredded red cabbage

2 carrots, shredded

1 zucchini, shredded

2 cups fresh arugula

1 cup fresh pea shoots (optional)

¼ cup roasted salted peanuts (optional)

Soy Lime Dressing (recipe follows; optional)

Oh, so you have some miso tahini sauce left over from the Grilled Salmon with Miso Tahini Sauce (page 205)? What else can you use it with? Don't despair because we are all about reusing, finding multiple uses for anything in our fridge, and spending our time wisely. Use the miso tahini sauce for our Malibu interpretation of pad thai, which naturally is vegan and gluten-free (although it goes great with salmon or shrimp). This is how we work less but eat better.

You'll see that this recipe calls for a soy lime dressing as well, but that's optional; you can totally make this dish with only the miso tahini sauce. If you do make the soy lime dressing for an additional punch of flavor, and you have leftovers, you can use the dressing as a marinade for chicken, steak, or fish.

Cook the noodles according to the package directions. Drain, and toss them in a medium bowl with 1 tablespoon olive oil. Then toss them with the Miso Tahini Sauce. Drain, dry, and cut the tofu into 1-inch cubes. In a medium skillet over high heat, add the remaining 1 tablespoon olive oil and sear the tofu on all sides, until browned, about 2 minutes per side.

Place the cabbage, carrots, zucchini, arugula, and pea shoots in a large bowl. Add the tofu and peanuts (if using). If you are using the Soy Lime Dressing, add it to the bowl and toss. If you are not using it, lightly dress the mixture with additional Miso Tahini Sauce.

Place the vegetable mixture on top of the noodles, and serve.

(RECIPE CONTINUES)

NOTE Although fish sauce has an expiration date, it lasts almost "forever" and makes a great addition to your fridge or pantry.

VEGAN OPTION Replace the fish sauce with a vegan brand, such as Ocean's Halo or VFISH.

SOY LIME DRESSING

MAKES 2 CUPS

1 cup fresh lime juice (about 4 limes)

⅓ cup soy sauce

¼ cup fish sauce (see Note)

¼ cup maple syrup

2 garlic cloves, grated

Red thai or Fresno chile peppers, sliced thin, to taste

3 tablespoons chopped fresh rosemary

Combine the lime juice, soy sauce, fish sauce, and maple syrup in a small bowl. Stir in the garlic, chile, and rosemary.

This dressing can be made up to 3 days in advance and stored covered in the refrigerator.

WHITE RICE
WITH FARRO AND QUINOA

SERVES 4

1 cup white jasmine rice (see Note)

1 cup quinoa (white, black, or tricolored)

1 cup farro or bulgur wheat

⅓ cup lemon dressing (see page 48)

2 tablespoons chopped fresh herbs

2 tablespoons chopped fresh chives

Salt to taste

Quick Faux Pickled Red Onions (recipe follows; optional)

I am slightly obsessed with grain mixes. I don't understand those popular diets of only meats and vegetables. Without grains or starch, I am starving! I like to keep a lot of cooked grains, beans, and lentils in the fridge and then combine them differently each day, but this particular combination I could eat every day of the week. I love the texture of quinoa and farro mixed with white rice.

Cook the rice, quinoa, and farro according to the package instructions.

In a medium bowl, combine the lemon dressing, herbs, chives, salt, and pickled onions (if using). Add the rice, quinoa, and farro, and toss.

You can eat this dish at room temperature or hot. To reheat it, you can microwave it or place it, covered, in a baking dish and heat it in a 375°F oven for 10 to 15 minutes, until heated through.

NOTE When I am in a rush, I cook my rice like pasta, in a large pot of salted water. When the rice is just done, I strain it, return it to the pot, and place it on the stove, burner off but still warm. I cover the pot with a lid and let it steam for about 10 minutes.

Combine rice and grains of your choice, such as brown rice with garbanzo beans and millet, or black rice with black lentils and black sesame seeds, then add fresh herbs and vegetables. Anything from cherry tomatoes to steamed green beans, sugar snap peas, asparagus, or roasted butternut squash goes great with a rice and grains salad combination.

QUICK FAUX PICKLED RED ONIONS

MAKES ¼ CUP IN A FLASH

Like "Peter Piper picked a peck of pickled peppers," the title of this recipe is a mouthful of nonsensical words. Yes, but have you made it? There are more intricate pickled onion recipes out there, but are there faster ones? This is a faux pickle, for when you want just a few tablespoons of not-raw onions with an acidic punch, but you don't want to spend much time making them, and you don't want a giant jar of pickled onions in your fridge that you may or may not ever finish.

¼ cup thinly sliced red onion

¼ teaspoon salt

1 tablespoon balsamic vinegar

A few tablespoons of very hot water

Place your sliced onion in a small bowl, sprinkle it with the salt, and drizzle a little balsamic vinegar over it—no need to measure, we need just a little bit, a splash, about a tablespoon. Give the onion a slight "massage" by rubbing the salt and vinegar into the slices. Then pour a few tablespoons of very hot water over it all and let it steep for about 3 minutes. Drain off the water and use your faux pickled onion. It will be more mellow and less sharp than raw onion, with minimal work.

NOTE Choosing your fish can be challenging. What is sustainable one day is no longer sustainable the next day. Check a sustainable seafood buying guide, such as SeafoodWatch.org, to stay in the know.

VEGAN OPTION Skip the fish, and grill blocks of tofu instead. Top them with the salad.

GRILLED FISH

WITH GREEK SALAD AND CRUDITÉS

SERVES 4

FISH

2 pounds fish fillets, such as Pacific halibut (see Note)

Salt and pepper

¼ cup lemon aioli (see page 219)

GREEK SALAD

1 basket halved cherry tomatoes (2 cups)

1 small cucumber, chopped

½ red onion, sliced thin

½ bell pepper, any color, chopped

½ cup kalamata or other olives, pitted

2 tablespoons capers

CRUDITÉS

1 small carrot, sliced thin

2 radishes, sliced thin

4 cooked baby potatoes, sliced thin

1 celery stalk, sliced thin

TO SERVE

Lemon dressing (see page 48)

1 teaspoon salt, or to taste

3 tablespoons fresh herbs (parsley, dill, cilantro, mint), for garnish

Summer sings the music of tomatoes, cucumbers, olives, and lemon juice. Sun, ocean breezes, and the flavors of Greece. This Greek salad with extra vegetables makes a refreshing topping on any fish.

I like to combine a healthy lean dish, such as this salad-topped grilled fish, with a creamy side, such as Sweet Corn Polenta (page 214). The white fish stands in for the feta cheese you'd typically find in a Greek salad, but if you want to add some feta, go ahead!

Fire up an outdoor grill to medium-high heat.

Season the fish fillets with salt and pepper, and coat them lightly with lemon aioli on both sides. Place the fillets on the grill, rounded side down, and cook until nice grill marks appear, about 5 minutes or until the fish easily lifts off the grill. Then turn them over to cook for another 5 minutes, until just cooked through. The aioli will prevent the fish from sticking. Transfer your grilled fish fillets to a serving platter.

In a large bowl, combine the Greek salad ingredients (tomatoes, cucumber, red onion, bell pepper, olives, and capers). Add the crudités ingredients (carrot, radishes, potatoes, celery), and toss with the lemon dressing. Season with the salt and garnish with the herbs. (You can do a traditional Greek salad with those ingredients only, but I recommend adding the crudités vegetables because more vegetables are more delicious and more colorful. Yes, I know crudités are traditionally all raw, but how *Swede* is it to add some cooked baby potatoes!)

SWEET CORN POLENTA

SERVES 6

1 cup polenta corn grits (my favorite brand is Bob's Red Mill Organic Corn Grits)

About ⅓ cup salted butter

2 teaspoons salt

4 cups fresh corn kernels, blanched or sautéed

Heavy cream to taste (¼ cup to 1¼ cups)

½ cup grated Parmesan cheese

2 tablespoons chopped fresh basil leaves

TIP: Use leftover polenta for a hybrid tamale quesadilla: Place a couple of tablespoons of cold polenta and some shredded cheese between 2 corn tortillas to make a quesadilla. Sauté the quesadilla in a little oil in a skillet over medium heat for a few minutes on both sides, until lightly browned and heated through. Serve with your favorite salsa.

Making polenta is uncomplicated and super comforting, and if you bake it, this dish will be an easy, breezy fast feast. Cooking it the traditional way on the stove includes a lot of constant stirring, which we don't have time for. This way, you'll place it in the oven and just check in every 15 minutes or so to stir. And it will overflow with fresh corn, basil, and Parmesan cheese.

Polenta is best held warm so that it remains soft. Once it cools down, it becomes stiffer. Polenta goes well with barbecued chicken and a green bean salad with cherry tomatoes.

Preheat the oven to 350°F.

In a standard 3-quart baking dish, combine 4 cups of water with the corn grits, 1 tablespoon of the butter, and the salt. (You do not need to blend the butter in, as it will melt once it is in the oven.) Place the baking dish in the oven and bake for about 45 minutes, stirring the polenta every 15 minutes.

After 45 minutes remove the dish from the oven and stir in the cooked corn, heavy cream to taste, more butter to taste, the Parmesan cheese, and fresh basil. Bake for an additional 10 minutes.

Serve immediately or cover and keep warm at a low temperature.

TWICE AS NICE ARTICHOKES + ARTICHOKE AIOLI

SERVES 2 TO 4

½ lemon or 3 tablespoons fresh lemon juice

Salt to taste

2 large artichokes, peeled, cleaned, and halved

¼ cup lemon dressing (see page 48) or reserved liquid from marinated artichoke hearts (see subrecipe)

Olive oil (optional)

Artichoke Aioli (recipe follows)

TIP Love artichokes? Try the raw artichoke salad on page 194.

Dipping artichokes in an artichoke aioli is definitely twice as nice. I love aioli with just about anything—I'd rather dip my fries (baked, of course) in aioli than in ketchup. This artichoke aioli is also amazing on a grilled fish sandwich.

Add the lemon half or juice to a large pot of salted water (to prevent oxidation and the artichokes turning brown), and bring to a boil. Add the artichokes and cook for about 15 minutes, or until they are just beginning to soften. Drain the artichokes and pat them dry.

Transfer the artichokes to a medium bowl and toss them with the lemon dressing or reserved liquid from marinated artichoke hearts. The artichoke hearts can be held in the dressing for a few days.

To serve, grill the artichoke hearts, or sear them in a little oil in a skillet over high heat, until they are reheated and slightly browned or charred. Serve with the Artichoke Aioli.

(RECIPE CONTINUES)

TIP Thin this aioli with the liquid from the marinated artichoke hearts or with some lemon dressing, and turn it into artichoke ranch dressing for the next day.

VEGAN OPTION Substitute vegan mayonnaise or vegan sour cream (see page 109) for the mayonnaise.

ARTICHOKE AIOLI

MAKES 1½ CUPS

1 (6-ounce) can or jar marinated artichoke hearts

1 cup mayonnaise, purchased or homemade (see below)

1 garlic clove, grated

Juice of ½ lemon

Salt to taste

¼ cup chopped fresh parsley

Drain and reserve the liquid from the marinated artichoke hearts. Combine the mayonnaise, artichoke hearts, garlic, lemon juice, salt, and parsley in a food processor. Whirl it all together until just blended but still chunky.

HOMEMADE MAYONNAISE

MAKES 1½ CUPS

Make your own mayo? Yeah, why not! And you can make a traditional version or vegan. Both are sides of the same coin; the only difference is whether you add eggs or soy milk or garbanzo bean liquid to the base.

MAYO BASE

1 cup light oil, such as sunflower or vegetable oil

2 teaspoons Dijon mustard

1 tablespoon white wine vinegar or lemon juice

½ teaspoon salt

1 large pasteurized egg (or two egg yolks)

OR

½ cup unflavored, unsweetened soy milk or garbanzo bean liquid

In a medium bowl, mix together the oil, mustard, vinegar, and salt to make the mayo base.

For traditional mayo, slowly whisk the mayo base into the egg until emulsified and thick; taste and adjust for seasoning. (If you don't want to use raw eggs, place your eggs in a small pan with the mustard, vinegar, and salt and a couple tablespoons of water; whisk vigorously over low heat until the egg starts to warm up, about 3 minutes, but before the eggs are scrambled. Remove from the heat and slowly whisk in the oil until thick and emulsified.)

For vegan mayo, add the soy milk or garbanzo bean liquid to the mayo base and use an immersion blender to mix until thick and delicious. Taste and adjust for seasoning.

I HEART YOU HAPPINESS AIOLI

MAKES 1 CUP

One *Urban Dictionary* definition of *aioli* is "an expression of extreme happiness." I agree! Traditionally it is a sauce made from olive oil, garlic, and salt, but today we mostly think of aioli as flavored mayonnaise. You can flavor an aioli many different ways, but the mother of all aiolis is the lemon aioli. Spicy (hot sauce) aioli is a top contender, however. From there let your heart and happiness be your guide.

Use aioli to coat vegetables, grilled cheese paninis (see page 89), or seafood (see page 111) before cooking.

1 cup mayonnaise, purchased or homemade (see opposite)

1 tablespoon fresh lemon juice (about ½ lemon), or hot sauce, curry, or seasoning of choice

1 garlic clove, grated

So easy: In a small bowl, stir together the mayonnaise, selected seasoning, and grated garlic. With lemon juice, it becomes lemon aioli; choose hot sauce, and it is spicy aioli; add curry powder, and it's curry aioli. Voilà!

TIP You can get creative here. Potential swaps for the lemon juice include hot sauce, Sriracha, paprika, soy sauce, curry, saffron, adobo sauce, spinach, kale, sun-dried tomatoes, cilantro, lime, rosemary, parsley, and . . . only a lack of imagination could stop the aioli creation.

VEGAN OPTION Substitute vegan mayonnaise if you like. Some vegan brands taste so good you practically can't tell the difference between them and traditional mayonnaise. My favorite vegan mayonnaise is Just Mayo. Or you could make your own (see recipe, opposite).

NOTE I used to always prefer flat-leaf parsley because I was led to believe it was better than curly. Then things started to change: The short film *Hair Love* won the Oscar, and for the first time I planted curly-leaf parsley in my garden beds. I can report that I had been missing out. Curls rule.

CHICKEN WITH GRAINY MUSTARD-ROSEMARY SAUCE

SERVES 4

4 skin-on "airline" chicken breasts

Salt to taste

Juice of ½ lemon

1 garlic clove, grated

1 tablespoon chopped fresh parsley (see Note)

Olive oil

GRAINY MUSTARD-ROSEMARY SAUCE

Juice of ½ lemon

3 tablespoons whole-grain mustard

1 garlic clove, grated

1 tablespoon chopped fresh rosemary

1 cup heavy cream

Salt to taste

TIP You can use the Grainy Mustard-Rosemary Sauce to make a potato or cauliflower gratin: Layer thinly sliced blanched potatoes or cauliflower florets with the sauce and some shredded Gruyère cheese (or your favorite cheese) in a baking dish, and bake at 350°F until bubbling for creamy mustard goodness.

I love mustard with my chicken. This sauce is a crowd-pleaser and so easy. You can use any part of the chicken that you like—skinless, boneless breast or chicken on the bone. I like skin-on "airline" chicken breasts a lot. They have the wing bone attached, which helps hold in the moisture of the breast meat.

Any time I serve something creamy like this dish, I like to pair it with something light such as kale salad, quinoa, or sauteed vegetables.

Preheat the oven to 375°F.

Season your chicken breasts lightly with salt, and toss them in a bowl with the lemon juice, garlic, and parsley.

Heat a little olive oil in a large skillet over medium heat, and sauté the chicken, skin-side down first, until it is browned and crispy on both sides, about 5 minutes. Transfer the chicken breasts to a sheet pan (reserve the skillet), place the sheet pan in the oven, and bake for about 10 minutes or until the chicken breasts are cooked through.

Once the chicken is cooked, transfer it to a serving platter and let it rest for a few minutes while you make the sauce.

Make the Grainy Mustard-Rosemary Sauce: In the same skillet in which you cooked the chicken, stir together the lemon juice, whole-grain mustard, garlic, and rosemary. Bring to a simmer and whisk in the heavy cream. Season to taste with salt.

To serve, pour the sauce over the chicken or serve it from a sauceboat.

EASY-PEASY VEGGIE CHICKEN STIR-FRY

SERVES 4

Olive or vegetable oil or 50/50 blend

1 small red onion, sliced

1 small red bell pepper, sliced

2 cups fresh green beans, trimmed

1 bunch fresh asparagus spears, trimmed

8 ounces (about 1 cup) mushrooms, sliced

1 cup broccoli florets

1 carrot, sliced into rounds

Salt to taste

2 skinless, boneless chicken breasts, sliced thin

Secret Stir-Fry Sauce (recipe follows)

½ cup chopped fresh parsley, for garnish

NOTE I usually start with the vegetables and do the chicken last, but you can do it in any order you like.

You can prepare this dish super-fast. It's full of vegetables and makes for an excellent meal, and leftovers heat up very well. The sauce ingredients are items that live in your fridge and pantry indefinitely (almost), probably don't involve shopping, and take only a few minutes to combine. You might need to buy the oyster sauce, but it keeps for a very long time in the fridge. If you make this recipe twice a year, you will probably use up the bottle before its expiration date.

The vegetables listed are only suggestions, so use your favorites. You can choose any protein—chicken, beef, fish, garbanzo beans, or tofu—for this dish. If you like a full serving of chicken per person, increase the number of chicken breasts to four. For a vegetarian version, skip the chicken and tweak the sauce by switching to vegan mushroom "oyster" sauce and vegetable broth.

Heat the oil in a large skillet (cast-iron if available) over medium-high heat for 1 to 2 minutes.

One at a time, sauté each vegetable separately in the skillet, tossing it frequently: red onion, bell pepper, green beans, asparagus, mushrooms, broccoli, and carrot. Salt them lightly as you go. When the vegetables are done (don't overcook them—keep them nice and crisp), transfer them to a medium bowl or serving platter. The cooking time will vary by vegetable, 3 to 5 minutes.

Next sauté the chicken slices until they are cooked all the way through, about 5 minutes. Transfer the chicken from the skillet to the same bowl or platter.

Pour the stir-fry sauce over the cooked vegetables and chicken, and garnish with the chopped parsley. This dish goes well with White Rice with Farro and Quinoa (page 210).

TIP I always keep fresh ginger in the freezer. It lasts until pretty much the end of time. Just take it out and grate off as much as you need (skin-on is fine) from the frozen chunk. Then back in the freezer it goes, patiently waiting for the next time you need it.

SECRET STIR-FRY SAUCE

MAKES 1½ CUPS

2 tablespoons cornstarch
2 tablespoons soy sauce
1 tablespoon grated fresh ginger (see Tip)
3 tablespoons oyster sauce
1 garlic clove, grated
Sliced fresh serrano or jalapeño chile peppers or red chili flakes to taste
1 cup chicken broth, homemade or purchased

In a small bowl, stir together the cornstarch, soy sauce, ginger, oyster sauce, garlic, chile or chili flakes, and chicken broth, making sure to dissolve the cornstarch. Pour the mixture into a skillet or small saucepan, and bring it to a light boil. (You can do this in the same skillet used to cook the vegetables and chicken.) Once the sauce changes color to a darker brown and begins to thicken, about 2 minutes, it is done.

THE REAL BIG STEAK

WITH SMOKY, SPICY BACON ADOBO BUTTER

SERVES 2 TO 4

1 (2-inch-thick) bone-in rib eye steak or other steak of your choice

Salt and pepper to taste

Oil

Smoky, Spicy Bacon Adobo Butter (page 227)

TIP Try the steak with the red or green chimichurri that accompanies our cauliflower steak (see page 107).

Once upon a time, when someone said "steak," we all knew what that meant, but now steak could be anything—cauliflower steak (see page 107), mushroom steak, tofu steak, seitan steak. The Impossible Steak isn't here yet, but we all know it is coming. That's great, but once in a blue Malibu moon we throw a "real" steak on the barbecue. All we do is sprinkle it with salt and serve it with seasoned butter. A thick cut of meat is hard to cook from start to finish on the grill without burning the exterior while the interior is still raw. The traditional restaurant and catering technique is to sear first and finish in the oven, but lately many chefs have tried the opposite, also known as the reverse sear, which is a great option for thicker cuts of meat. Try both methods and see which you prefer.

We add lots of vegetables and healthy grains to the meal, such as cauliflower "potatoes" (see page 118), Delicata Squash with Red Lentils (page 104), or grilled kale (see page 193). More vegetables for everyone, one dinner at a time.

Let the steak come to room temperature. This will take about 30 minutes for a refrigerated steak. It is a thick cut of meat, so you can season the steak liberally with salt and pepper. Then choose to sear first or sear last.

(RECIPE CONTINUES)

TIP Make a spicy finishing salt to kick this dish up one more notch. Combine 1 cup flaky sea salt, such as Maldon, with 1 tablespoon adobo sauce and stir until combined. Allow the salt to dry, and then store and use as finishing salt.

Sear-first method: Preheat the oven to 400°F. Sear the steak with a little oil in a hot cast-iron skillet, or alternatively grill on the barbecue until it is nice and charred on both sides. You can sear the steak ahead of time, and chill and keep in the fridge overnight. This is how steak is often prepared for off-site catering events. When you are ready to finish the steak, bring to room temperature and place in a heat-proof pan and roast in the oven until it reaches the desired internal temperature (130°F for medium-rare, 140°F for medium, and 150°F for medium-well), 10 to 15 minutes, depending on the thickness of the steak.

Sear-last method: Preheat the oven to 250°F. Place the seasoned steak on a small rack on top of a rimmed sheet pan, and bake it in the oven for about 1 hour, until it reaches an internal temperature of 115°F to 125°F. Remove the pan from the oven and transfer the steak either to a preheated skillet with a little oil or to a barbecue grill. Sear both sides over high heat until the meat is browned and crisp, about 1 minute per side, or until it reaches the desired internal temperature (130°F for medium-rare, 140°F for medium, and 150°F for medium-well).

Once your steak is cooked to the desired temperature, transfer it to a cutting board and spread it generously with the Smoky, Spicy Bacon Adobo Butter (or with a seasoned butter of your choice). Let it rest for a few minutes while the buttery goodness melts.

SEASONED BUTTERS

(YOUR SECRET WEAPON)

Keep your freezer stocked with seasoned butter, and dinner is as easy as can be. You can roll up the butters in parchment paper like cute little gifts or fill a butter crock to use at that time or freeze for later. Allow the frozen butter to come to room temperature before using.

These are all great not only with steak, chicken, and fish, but also with veggies.

NOTE Use leftover canned chiles in adobo sauce to make adobo aioli (see page 219), Charred Salsa Roja (page 271), or Roasted Tomato Coulis with canned chiles in adobo sauce (page 178).

SMOKY, SPICY BACON ADOBO BUTTER

MAKES ABOUT ¾ CUP

8 tablespoons (1 stick) salted butter, at room temperature

¼ cup cooked bacon bits (about 3 slices)

2 tablespoons sauce from canned chiles in adobo sauce (or to taste—more for more spicy, less for mild)

Blend the butter, bacon bits, and adobo sauce in a food processor until smooth. Form the mixture into a log.

BLUE CHEESE BUTTER

MAKES ABOUT 1½ CUPS

1 cup crumbled blue cheese

8 tablespoons (1 stick) salted butter, at room temperature

2 tablespoons Worcestershire sauce

Combine the blue cheese, butter, and Worcestershire sauce in a food processor and blend until smooth. Form into a log.

(RECIPE CONTINUES)

LEMON CAPER BUTTER

MAKES ABOUT 1½ CUPS

8 tablespoons (1 stick) salted butter, at room temperature

⅓ cup capers

1 garlic clove, grated

⅓ cup chopped fresh herbs of your choice

Zest from 1 small lemon

3 tablespoons fresh lemon juice

2 tablespoons crème fraîche (optional)

Place the butter, capers, garlic, herbs, lemon zest and juice, and crème fraîche (if using) in a food processor, and use the pulse feature to process until they are just blended. Do not over-blend. There should be speckles of capers and herbs. Form the mixture into a log. Great sole solution, the easiest sole "meunière" à la minute.

NOTE You can sub pickled sushi ginger if preferred.

GREAT GINGER BUTTER

MAKES ABOUT ¾ CUP

8 tablespoons (1 stick) salted butter, at room temperature

3 tablespoons thinly sliced fresh ginger (see Note)

2 garlic cloves, sliced thin

1 tablespoon thinly sliced green onions (scallions)

Melt 1 tablespoon of the butter in a small skillet over medium heat. Add the ginger and garlic, and cook until translucent, about 4 minutes. Remove the skillet from the heat and allow to cool, about 5 minutes.

Place the cooked ginger-garlic mixture, the remaining 7 tablespoons butter, and the green onion in a food processor, and use the pulse feature to process until just blended. Do not over-blend. There should be speckles of ginger and garlic. Form the mixture into a log.

GRANDMA'S BRISKET

WITH ONION GRAVY

SERVES 6 TO 8

1 5- to 6-pound brisket

Salt and pepper

Olive oil

4 large yellow onions, chopped

6 garlic cloves, left whole

Fresh herbs of your choice, such as parsley or thyme sprigs

2 tablespoons paprika

½ cup balsamic vinegar

1 cube concentrated organic chicken bouillon (Kallo is my favorite brand)

4 cups beef stock, purchased or homemade

Horseradish Cream (page 56), for serving (optional)

I love this traditional recipe. Back in my private chef days, I cooked brisket all the time. It takes a while in the oven, but it is the easiest party meal to serve, with no last-minute prep or cooking—only heating. You can make it days in advance, and you can also freeze it.

A brisket has two cuts, separated by a layer of fat. The first cut is pretty much all muscle and little fat, and is usually thinner and flatter than the second cut (a.k.a. the point cut), which has more fat and could be considered more flavorful. I usually purchase the first cut, because it is more even in thickness, is easier to cover with broth, but you can use either cut here; the brisket is braised in this recipe, so it'll turn out tender and flavorful either way.

Preheat the oven to 375°F.

Season your brisket generously with salt and pepper, and then—this is important—brown it well. Do this in any way that is easiest for you. You can heat 2 tablespoons olive oil in a large cast-iron skillet and sear the meat on both sides until well browned, about 8 minutes per side. If the brisket is too large to fit in your skillet, no problem: place the brisket on a preheated barbecue grill instead. Once your brisket is well browned on both sides, place it in a baking dish.

Heat 3 tablespoons olive oil in a large skillet over medium heat. The heat should not be too high, just nice and medium. Add your chopped onions and cook, stirring a few times, until they are brown all over, but not so much that they

(RECIPE CONTINUES)

NOTE The brisket covered in the gravy will keep for 5 days in the fridge. It can also be frozen covered in the gravy.

TIP What can you do with the rendered brisket fat? Fat is fat and you can use it to sauté or fry, just like any oil. Potatoes are always a good choice.

become caramelized, about 8 minutes. Add the whole garlic cloves and cook for another 1 to 2 minutes. Season your onion-garlic mixture with 2 teaspoons of salt, and add the herbs, paprika, vinegar, bouillon cube, and ½ cup of water to the pan. Stir the mixture, and then add it to the brisket in the baking dish. Pour the beef stock over the brisket. Ideally, your dish is nice and snug because your brisket needs to be completely covered with liquid. If the baking pan is much larger than the brisket, you may need more broth to cover the brisket.

Cover the pan with foil, and bake in the oven for about 5 hours. This is what is referred to as braising: searing first and then slowly cooking in liquid. We want the brisket to be so soft that it is falling apart. If it is not soft, leave it in there longer, make sure it is covered, and add more beef broth if needed. You can turn the brisket over midway as well to ensure it is evenly cooked on both sides.

Once it is cooked and soft, gently remove the brisket from the broth, place it on a rimmed sheet pan, and chill it overnight. (Do not attempt to slice it when it is hot because it will fall apart. If you want to eat it right away, shred it rather than slice it.)

Transfer the broth, with the onions, from the baking pan to a container, such as a 2-quart bowl, and keep it in the fridge overnight.

The next day, preheat the oven to 375°F.

The chilled brisket will be easy to cut into thin or thick slices. Transfer the sliced brisket to a baking dish, preferably one that can serve as a serving dish.

Remove the broth from the fridge. A layer of fat should have risen to the surface. Scrape off the fat and save it for other uses (see Tip). Blend the onions and defatted broth into a thick gravy using either a blender, a food processor, or an

(RECIPE CONTINUES)

immersion blender. The onions will thicken the gravy, so no flour or cornstarch is needed. If the gravy is too thin, sauté more onions, add them to the broth, and blend again. Taste for seasoning and add salt as needed. Pour the gravy over the sliced brisket. Reheat the gravy-covered brisket in the oven for 20 minutes or until warmed through.

Serve the brisket with the Horseradish Cream alongside.

BAKED SWEET POTATO FRIES

SERVES 4

4 sweet potatoes

Olive oil or canola oil

1 cup Pucker Up Tahini Sauce (page 278)

1 cup Crispy Garbanzo Beans (page 273)

¼ cup chopped fresh parsley, for garnish (optional)

½ cup pomegranate seeds (optional)

TIP Instead of the tahini dressing, try drizzling the sweet potatoes with lime dressing (see page 48) or Lime Cucumber Yogurt Sauce (page 277). Drizzling them with plain vegan yogurt is also yum yum. Of course, nobody is going to stop you from enjoying the fried sweet potatoes in their simple glory, without any embellishment.

NOTE Don't feel like making fries? Bake the potatoes whole for about 1 hour, or until soft when pierced. Slice them open lengthwise and drizzle the inside with the tahini sauce, and garnish with the garbanzo beans, parsley, and pomegranate seeds.

Baked sweet potato fries, yes, please. I can eat them all day every day. To get them nicely golden-brown and crisp, do not crowd your sheet pans. To make fries for a crowd, you need to work with several sheet pans at a time.

Use any kind of sweet potato or yam. My favorite readily available variety is the garnet yam. Try this recipe with purple yams or white Japanese sweet potatoes.

Preheat the oven to 400°F.

First we need to zebra-peel the skin on our sweet potatoes. A little skin holds the sweet potatoes together; too much skin gets chewy. With a vegetable peeler, peel the potatoes in lengthwise strips, removing half the skin. Then cut the sweet potatoes into wedges, 4 to 6 wedges per half potato, depending on how thick you cut them. Place the wedges on a sheet pan that is greased with olive oil or canola oil. Do not crowd your pan.

Bake for about 8 minutes, or until the underside is browned and crisp. Turn the fries over to brown the other side, about 5 minutes. Remove and dry the sweet potato fries on paper towels.

To serve the sweet potatoes, drizzle them with the Pucker Up Tahini Sauce and Crispy Garbanzo Beans. Garnish with the parsley and pomegranate seeds, if using.

THE GOOD STUFFING

SERVES 4 TO 6

4 cups (1-inch) cubes or chunks of corn bread or corn muffins (see Note)

1½ cups fresh corn kernels

2 tablespoons salted butter

1 bell pepper, chopped (any color)

½ yellow onion, chopped

1 celery stalk, sliced

4 apples, peeled, cored, and cut into chunks

About 6 strips julienne sliced bacon, cooked until crisp (¾ cup; see Note, page 45)

½ cup chopped fresh parsley

½ cup dried cranberries

¾ cup turkey (or chicken) drippings or broth (optional)

NOTE Go ahead and make your corn bread from scratch, but I am going to buy mine. If you want to make your own, however, bake it ahead of time and freeze it. Nothing but craziness is accomplished by doing too much on the same day, especially if that day is Thanksgiving. The stuffing will not be any better because the bread is fresh.

TIP Can you stuff your stuffing into a mini-pumpkin? Yes! So cute (see page 238).

I don't believe in stuffing turkey or chicken, because it slows down the cooking process and makes it harder to get everything cooked evenly. This stuffing bakes separately—so why call it stuffing? Because we put good stuff in it!

Preheat the oven to 400°F.

Place the corn bread cubes or chunks in a baking dish.

In a medium skillet over high heat, cook the corn in 1 tablespoon of the butter for about 2 minutes, until just beginning to soften. Remove the corn from the skillet and add it to the corn bread. Then, in the same skillet, cook the bell pepper, onion, and celery together until they are just beginning to soften, 2 to 3 minutes. Transfer the vegetables to the baking dish. Last, cook the apples, using the remaining 1 tablespoon butter. Sauté the apples for about 5 minutes, until lightly browned. When they are done, transfer them to the baking dish as well.

Add the bacon, parsley, and cranberries to the corn bread mixture, and toss lightly without breaking the bread into a mess.

Bake for about 20 minutes. In the last 5 minutes of baking time, add some turkey or chicken drippings or broth if using.

HOLIDAY HEALTHY GRAINS

SERVES 6

1 leek

1 tablespoon salted butter

Salt to taste

1 cup dried cranberries

½ cup roasted sliced skin-on almonds

2 tablespoons chopped fresh parsley

1 cup wild rice, cooked according to the package instructions (see Note)

2 cups quinoa, cooked according to the package instructions (see Note)

2 cups Cubed Roasted Butternut Squash (page 54)

¼ cup lemon dressing (see page 48)

Jack Be Little Mini Pumpkins (recipe follows; optional)

NOTE Cook quinoa and wild rice until at least 50 percent of the grain has "bloomed" (opened).

TIP Use any grain, lentil, or bean combination that suits you. Use what you have and what you like. Cherry tomatoes, asparagus, and green beans are all delicious additions.

The holidays are here and our holiday table is almost complete. We have traditional turkey (see my first book, *Malibu Farm Cookbook,* page 250), The Good Stuffing (page 236), and brisket (page 229). We need sweet potatoes, so we will choose one: mashed sweet potatoes, also in *Malibu Farm Cookbook,* page 115, or sweet potato fries (page 235). But we need more. The Malibu Farm choice to serve with your sweet potatoes is couscous, wild rice, or any other nicely crunchy grain.

At Christmas I like to work with the traditional colors, red and green—but by no means are they the only colors of the holiday season. Your holiday, your colors. Find the gift of nature that best represents your holiday rainbow.

Thinly slice the whole leek—yes, the dark green leaves too—into rings and discard the root end. (There is no reason to toss out half of the leek because it is darker. The dark part is still delicious; it just takes a little longer to cook and to soften. When you're slicing, keep the light and dark parts separate.) Leeks can have soil deep inside them, so submerge the sliced leek in a bowl of cold water to wash it well. Dry on paper towels before cooking.

In a medium skillet, melt the butter over low heat. Add the darker parts of the sliced leek first and sauté for 3 minutes. Then add the rest of the leek (the white end), and cook for an additional 3 minutes, until all of the leek is soft, about 6 minutes total. Season with salt. In a large bowl, combine

(RECIPE CONTINUES)

the leeks with the cranberries, almonds, parsley, wild rice and quinoa, and cooked butternut squash. Drizzle in the lemon dressing, and toss. Serve in the bowl or stuff into the mini pumpkins.

The stuffing can be made up to 2 days in advance.

TIP Save the scooped-out pumpkin seeds, rinse them, and dry them. Then eat them or plant them.

JACK BE LITTLE MINI PUMPKINS

Mini pumpkins are in every store, everywhere, around Halloween. They will last until the holidays, especially if you keep them in the fridge. Jack Be Little are the orange ones and Baby Boo the white ones, and obviously we will need some of both.

Roast the pumpkins in a preheated 375°F oven for 40 minutes or until they are just soft and you can pierce through them with a sharp knife. Remove them from the oven and allow them to cool. Then cut off the tops of the pumpkins and scoop out the seeds (see Tip).

The pumpkins can be prepared up to 2 days in advance and kept chilled.

To serve stuffed with Holiday Healthy Grains (page 239), heat the filled pumpkins in a 375°F oven for 20 minutes before serving. You can also stuff these babies with Pumpkin Chocolate Bread Pudding (page 151) or sweet potato mash (in *Malibu Farm Cookbook*, page 115).

RED AND GREEN HOLIDAY BEANS

SERVES 4

Salt to taste

2 cups fresh green beans

¼ cup olive oil

⅓ cup black lentils, cooked according to the package instructions, drained

2 tablespoons lemon dressing (see page 48)

1 small pickled red chile pepper, sliced thin (optional; see page 113)

1 red bell pepper, roasted and marinated (recipe follows)

1 basket cherry tomatoes, halved (2 cups)

¼ cup chopped fresh dill or other fresh herb of choice, for garnish

NOTE Both the lentils (cooked and tossed in lemon dressing and salt) and the roasted and marinated red bell pepper can be made several days in advance.

I love holiday colors for my holiday table, and one of my favorite vegetable side dishes is green beans with roasted and marinated red bell peppers. It's super easy to make ahead, with zero last-minute prep, and is served at room temperature, so it's great for a crowd.

Because my youngest child has been vegetarian forever, I often add beans or lentils to my vegetable side dishes for a boost of protein. I use black lentils here, but any color would work; try red, yellow, green, or brown.

Bring a large pot of salted water to a boil, add the green beans, and blanch them for about 2 minutes. Remove them from the water and let them cool on a sheet pan. (Unless you are cooking large quantities of green beans, there is no need to drop them into ice water. The beans actually taste better when they are allowed to air-dry, rather than absorb more water by cooling in ice.) In a large bowl, lightly toss the beans with the olive oil and salt.

Season the cooked lentils with the lemon dressing and salt to taste, and add the chile pepper if using. Combine the lentils, roasted and marinated red bell pepper, and cherry tomatoes with the green beans. Garnish with the dill or other herbs of choice.

Serve at room temperature.

(RECIPE CONTINUES)

ROASTED AND MARINATED RED BELL PEPPERS

MAKES 2 PEPPERS

2 red bell peppers

2 tablespoons olive oil

2 garlic cloves, sliced thin

Salt to taste

2 tablespoons balsamic vinegar

½ teaspoon Worcestershire sauce (optional)

There are several ways to roast your red bell peppers. If you have a gas stove, turn a burner on high, lay the peppers directly over the flame, and roast, turning them occasionally, until the skin is completely charred. If you do not have a gas stove, then you can put the peppers under the oven broiler or on a barbecue grill; turn them a few times until they are charred black on all sides.

Once the skin is charred, place the red peppers in a bowl and cover it with a plate or a pot lid (or, less ideally, plastic wrap). We just need the peppers to steam for a few minutes. Once they have steamed, peel off the charred skin and slice the peppers into strips. Place them in a bowl or other container.

In a small skillet, heat the olive oil over medium-low heat, and cook the thin garlic slices until they just turn brown. Pour the garlic over the red bell pepper strips and season them lightly with salt. Add the balsamic vinegar and Worcestershire sauce. Use the marinated peppers right away or store in the fridge for up to 5 days.

CHARRED OCTOPUS

WITH POBLANO SALSA

SERVES 2 TO 4

1 tablespoon whole black peppercorns

6 fresh bay leaves

1 (6-pound) cleaned octopus

1 whole lemon cut in half

Roasted Poblano Sauce (recipe follows)

NOTE I suggest serving this with roasted Romanesco and with shaved raw Brussels sprouts.

This recipe is from the shores of Miami Beach and our chef team there. Often guests confuse calamari with octopus, but they are not the same thing. Calamari is squid. Octopus is, well, octopus. Both are mollusks but squid swim in the open sea, sometimes alone and sometimes in groups, while octopus are loners that live on the sea floor. Both can camouflage themselves by swimming fast and shooting ink.

Fill a large pot (8 to 12 quarts) halfway with water, add the peppercorns and bay leaves, and bring to a boil.

Take the cleaned octopus and rinse it with fresh water. To tenderize the octopus, dip it in the boiling water, remove it at once, wait for the water to return to boiling and dip it briefly again, repeat this process one more time, for a total of three times, until the tentacles have curled. Then add the octopus to the water and simmer until it is tender, 35 to 45 minutes.

Remove the octopus from the water, put it on a sheet pan, and chill it in the refrigerator for about 30 minutes.

After the octopus has cooled, remove the head and discard it. Cut off each tentacle. Lay the tentacles on a cutting board, and with a small knife score both sides of each tentacle above the suction cup to remove the top flesh layer. Discard the skin. Squeeze lemon juice over the tentacles.

(RECIPE CONTINUES)

Heat a barbecue grill to high. When it is hot, grill the tentacles until they are charred and heated through, about 8 minutes. When the octopus has nice grill marks, put it in a bowl, add the Roasted Poblano Sauce, toss, and then put it on a serving plate.

ROASTED POBLANO SAUCE

MAKES 2 CUPS

2 medium poblano chile peppers
1 tablespoon minced garlic
2 medium shallots, minced
1 bunch fresh parsley, minced, about 2 cups
1 cup olive oil
1 teaspoon ground cumin
2 tablespoons fresh lemon juice
1 teaspoon salt

Preheat the oven to 500°F.

Place the poblano peppers on a sheet pan and roast until they are dark, 8 to 15 minutes. Once they are done, remove them from the oven, put them in a bowl, and cover it with a lid or (less ideal) plastic wrap. Let the chiles steam for 2 to 5 minutes.

Remove the skin and the seeds from the roasted poblanos, and cut the chiles into a small dice. Place them in a bowl, add the garlic, shallots, parsley, olive oil, cumin, lemon juice, and salt, and mix until all are fully incorporated.

AVOCADO PIZZA

SERVES 2 TO 4
(MAKES TWO 8-INCH PIZZAS)

Flour, for the work surface

2 (7-ounce) balls of pizza dough, ready to bake, purchased or homemade (see page 254)

Ricotta Cream (recipe follows)

3 avocados, sliced thin

1 serrano chile pepper, sliced thin

2 tablespoons agave nectar

Pinch of coarse sea salt

2 tablespoons chopped fresh cilantro

1 lime, cut into quarters

NOTE In Malibu we make a green quesadilla version of this recipe, using a spinach tortilla, with melted pepper Jack cheese, sliced avocado, serrano chiles, cilantro, salt, and lime juice. It is served with Kale Apple Serrano Hot Sauce (page 61) and honey.

Miami was our second out-of-state location to open in, but it ran almost three years behind schedule, and many times I doubted it would ever actually happen. The opening date was scheduled and published again and again, but each time last-minute permit issues put a halt to our Miami Beach dreams. When we finally passed inspection and opened on Earth Day 2018, it felt like a gift from Mother Earth herself.

All our restaurants have local specials and dishes unique to them, and our Miami location has a wood-burning pizza oven. For many years we tried to get a pizza oven permit in Malibu but never succeeded, and so we are super jealous of Miami. But we did learn that we can still make this pizza even without a pizza oven, and so can you at home. I am including the Miami crust recipe on page 254, but you can use a store-bought crust, toasted pita bread, or baked puff pastry instead. Additionally you can also convert this recipe into a quesadilla (see Note), which is what we did in Malibu because we do not have a pizza oven on the pier and a lot of our guests requested the Miami pizza.

This pizza is a Miami Beach dream. And for both this pizza and the Greek salad pizza (see page 253), you bake the crust without toppings, which is especially easy on the barbecue grill. All the Miami pizzas are created by our local team, led by Executive Chef Thomas Buckley and Chef de Cuisine Yanelquis Penton.

(RECIPE CONTINUES)

Preheat the oven to 500°F or the highest setting, or heat a barbecue grill.

Lightly flour a work surface, then roll out your pizza dough to form two 8-inch rounds, although dough in an imperfect rustic shape is perfectly all right as well. Bake your naked pizza crusts on a pizza stone in the oven, one at a time, or grill the crusts on the barbecue on both sides until cooked through. Depending on the heat of your oven, this will take about 10 minutes. On the barbecue grill, this will take about 5 minutes per side. How do you know when your crust is cooked? Look at the bottom, which should be well browned and crispy. If it is still pale and soft, cook it for a few more minutes.

Spread a generous amount of the Ricotta Cream over each cooked pizza crust. Top with the sliced avocados and serrano pepper. Drizzle with the agave nectar, sprinkle with sea salt, and top with the cilantro and lime slices.

RICOTTA CREAM

MAKES 3 CUPS

4 jalapeño peppers, seeded

1 serrano chile pepper, seeded

2 cups ricotta cheese, purchased or homemade (see page 117)

¼ cup crème fraîche or sour cream

Juice of 2 lemons

Pinch of salt

Combine the jalapeños, serrano chile, ricotta, crème fraîche, lemon juice, and salt in a blender or food processor, and blend until smooth. This can be made 1 day in advance and stored in the fridge.

GREEK SALAD PIZZA

SERVES 2 TO 4
(MAKES TWO 8-INCH PIZZAS)

Flour for the work surface

2 (7-ounce) balls of pizza dough, purchased or homemade (see page 254)

1 cup hummus, purchased or homemade (see Note)

Greek salad (see page 213)

1 cup crumbled feta cheese

NOTE There's a hummus recipe in my first book, *Malibu Farm Cookbook*, page 79.

VEGAN OPTION Skip the feta cheese and enjoy a vegan pizza instead.

This is the pizza version of our omelet salads, and I hope you start to play with both your pizzas and your omelets by adding lots of salads to both. I have a pizza oven in my backyard, which my husband built. He said he was going to be a pizza master, and I had all sorts of fantasies that I would come home from work and there he would be in his apron, making pizzas for me and offering me a glass of rosé.

Yeah, that never happened. I think he made pizza twice and then said it was too much work, but let's see if maybe one day he will fire up the oven again. Hope lives, and I hope you are inclined to make pizza often. If making the dough is too much work, skip it and use toasted pita bread instead!

Preheat the oven to 500°F or the highest setting, or heat a barbecue grill.

Lightly flour a work surface, then roll out your pizza dough to form two 8-inch rounds, although dough in an imperfect rustic shape is perfectly all right as well. Bake your naked pizza crusts on a pizza stone in the oven, one at a time, or grill your naked pizza crusts on the barbecue on both sides until cooked through. Depending on the heat of your oven, this will take about 10 minutes. On the barbecue grill, this will take about 5 minutes per side. How do you know when your crust is cooked? Look at the bottom, which should be well browned and crispy. If it is still pale and soft, cook it for a few more minutes.

Once the crusts are baked, remove them from the oven, spread them with the hummus, and top them with the Greek salad and a generous amount of feta cheese.

MIAMI HOMEMADE PIZZA DOUGH

MAKES TWELVE 7-OUNCE BALLS

7¼ cups (58 ounces) Antimo Caputo 00 flour (see Note, plus more for the work surface)

½ cup (4 ounces) Caputo Heart of Cereals multigrain mixture (see Note)

3 tablespoons (1½ ounces) salt

1¾ cups (14 fluid ounces) water

1 tablespoon (½ ounce) dry yeast

2 tablespoons (1 fluid ounce) olive oil, plus extra for coating the dough

2 tablespoons (1 fluid ounce) agave nectar

NOTE Caputo 00 flour is considered by many a "choice" brand for pizza, but you can substitute any 00 flour available at your local market. Caputo Heart of Cereals is a selection of cereals and seeds: sunflower, rye, flax, barley, sesame, and wheat. If you can't find it, substitute whole-wheat flour and 2 tablespoons of coarsely ground sunflower and sesame seeds.

We tested a lot of recipes for the Miami pizzas. We wanted something whole-wheaty, hearty, and healthy but still accessible to most guests. Nobu Executive Chef Thomas Buckley nailed this crust, made with wheat flour, grains, and agave. The crust looks gorgeous, is healthy, and tastes delicious. You will need a 6-quart bowl to fit all at once.

In a large mixing bowl, combine the Caputo 00 flour, Heart of Cereals, and salt.

In a small bowl, combine the water with the dry yeast, the 2 tablespoons olive oil, and the agave. (The agave activates the dry yeast.) Let it sit for 5 minutes.

In a standing mixer fitted with the dough hook, combine the wet ingredients (the yeast mixture) with the dry ingredients (flour, Heart of Cereals, salt) until the dough forms a ball. Remove the bowl from the mixer, glaze the dough with olive oil, and cover the bowl with a lid or (less ideal) plastic wrap. Let the dough rest for 30 minutes in the mixing bowl.

Weigh out a dozen 7-ounce dough balls and place them on a nonstick sheet pan. Cover the dough balls with a lightweight kitchen towel or (less ideal) plastic wrap, and place the pan in the refrigerator to let the dough rest for 24 hours.

Place a round ceramic pizza stone in the oven and heat the oven to 500°F.

Take the pizza dough from the refrigerator. (If you won't be using all 12 balls, wrap the extras in plastic wrap and store them in the freezer. They will keep frozen for several weeks; defrost overnight before using.) Place the dough on a floured surface for stretching. Stretch the pizza balls by hand, one by one, until they are evenly thin throughout.

One at a time, place a stretched pizza dough on a pizza paddle. Use a tablespoon to pour 1 to 2 spoonfuls of oil on top of the dough, and spread it out evenly. Slide the oiled dough onto the rack in the oven, and bake until golden brown, 3 to 5 minutes (rotate it inside the oven to ensure even baking).

Remove the dough from the oven when it has developed a nice brown color. Set aside. Repeat the process for each ball.

SKÅL!

AFTER-DINNER DRINKS

AND SNACKS

When I first moved to **MALIBU,** I was baffled by the darkness. Why no streetlights? So dangerous to drive. Where were the landscape lights? The lights on the high school football field? How can the kids play Friday night football? Having been a resident of Los Angeles for more than two decades I was now a **BIG-CITY GIRL,** and this seemed like an obvious problem that needed fixing.

"**LOOK UP,**" someone said.

When I lived in Hollywood, I saw plenty of stars posing on red carpets while cameras flashed. But here, viewed from a residential street in Malibu, there were actual **STARS** lighting up **THE SKY, THE UNIVERSE, AND BEYOND.** Stars that took your breath away, stars with names you had never learned, knowledge you had to earn, the biggest stars in our universe right there, **EVERYWHERE,** all the time, **UNTIL THE END OF TIME.** Yeah, the country folks in Malibu were right. The only stars that matter come out at night.

And as we look to the **FUTURE,** we see a future with more **GRAINS AND GREENS,** less meat and animal products, we imagine a world with less plastic and less waste. You may say we are **MALIBU DREAMERS,** but we see more **INCLUSION** and less division, we hope for women's rights, human rights, and animal rights, we imagine us all **LIVING IN PEACE.**

And as the sun dips below the horizon we hope to see it rise yet another day, but we know that **TOMORROW IS NEVER PROMISED.** That is all right, because tonight as we stare at the **MOON AND STARS,** we will **SKÅL** and drink **TO OUR HEALTH** with rhubarb-scented aquavit and we will drink **FOR OUR HEALTH** with beet juice mockmosas

FROZEN ROSÉ COCKTAIL

SERVES 6

¾ bottle (500 ml) rosé wine

3 fluid ounces vodka

2 cups frozen strawberries

3 fluid ounces peach liqueur (optional)

½ cup agave nectar, or to taste

½ cup fresh grapefruit juice

½ cup fresh lemon juice

Life is better through rosé-colored glasses. Much better. We have a slushy machine in our restaurants, but we are not going to stop our f'rosé fun just because there is no frozen slushy machine at home. Frozen strawberries will create the slushy texture and the pretty pink color.

This drink was originally brought to us by our Miami team; David Shoham, our beverage director and opening general manager, created the home version of the recipe.

TIP Freeze these babies into ice pops. Use push-up ice-pop bags, as this will freeze on the softer side. Or, if you can only find an ice-pop mold, reduce the vodka to 2 fluid ounces and the liqueur to ½ ounce; the smaller amount of alcohol will let the mixture freeze.

Combine the rosé, vodka, strawberries, peach liqueur (if using), agave, and grapefruit and lemon juices in a blender, and blend well. Now let's get the party started. Pink-striped paper straws recommended. Because more pink is more fun.

RHUBARB-INFUSED AQUAVIT

MAKES 15 SHOTS (SERVES A PARTY)

1 teaspoon fennel seeds

1 teaspoon caraway seeds

1 (750-ml) bottle vodka

1 teaspoon white or brown sugar

3 whole rhubarb stalks, cut in chunks

3 tablespoons whole pink peppercorns

3 fresh mint sprigs

When the night ends and we wonder what tomorrow holds, we can toast the future and lift a glass of *skål*. Tonight, under the moonlight, we cherish what we have, which is a bottle of beautifully infused vodka, reminding us of exactly how lucky we are.

Rhubarb is very popular in Sweden, but if you have trouble finding it, you can skip it. Aquavit is a Scandinavian distilled spirit that is seasoned with various spices, herbs, and citrus; you can also use it as the base spirit for many cocktails.

In a small dry skillet over medium heat, toast the fennel and caraway seeds for 1 to 2 minutes; allow to cool. Combine the vodka, sugar, rhubarb, peppercorns, fennel and caraway seeds, and mint sprigs in a large pitcher, and let infuse at room temperature for 2 weeks.

Strain the infused aquavit into a pitcher. When ready to serve, fill individual shot glasses and raise your glasses to the past, to the future, and to right now.

DISTILLERY

MIMOSA RAINBOW FLIGHT

SERVES 7

For each glass, add
2 tablespoons of juice of choice: watermelon juice, kale juice, apple juice, green juice, orange juice, beet juice, or grapefruit juice

1 bottle champagne (or sparkling white grape juice for mockmosas)

Should a mimosa only be made with orange juice? No, a mimosa can sparkle with every flavor and every color of the rainbow. Here's a whole rainbow of mimosas.

Bring out seven individual flutes, coup glasses, or any glass you like, add a dash of different colorlful juice to each, and fill them high with lots of bubbles.

COCONUT HORCHATA

MAKES 4 QUARTS

2 cups coconut milk (see Tip)

1 cup rice (white, green bamboo, or brown)

1 cup unsalted raw almonds, walnuts, or cashews

1 cup pitted Medjool dates or dried figs

½ cup chopped black kale (optional, for green rice version)

½ cup maple syrup, or honey, to taste

½ tablespoon vanilla extract

Sprinkle of ground cinnamon

TIP No coconut milk? Just use 1 cup of sweetened coconut flakes. Or you can make coconut milk by blending 2 cups shredded coconut flakes with 4 cups hot water, then strain out the pulp. Want to go one extra step? Save the coconut pulp, spread it on a sheet pan, and dry in the lowest setting on your oven for about 4 hours. Once it is completely dry, whirl in a food processor until it turns into a fine flour, and you just made coconut milk and coconut flour from a bag of shredded coconut flakes that was in your pantry for too long.

To milk or not to milk. If we are talking about goats, no. I milked our lady goat for a few months. Unless you are a pro and have pro equipment, it's a lot of work with very little reward. Making nut, rice, or oat milk is significantly easier and faster.

Horchata, a classic Mexican drink made with water, rice, sugar, and cinnamon, is offered almost daily for staff family meals on the pier. It is traditionally made with long-grain white rice, but you can use any rice. Brown rice gives it a nutty flavor, but my favorite is using green bamboo rice with a handful of kale. You can also use oats, regular or gluten-free, instead of rice. I don't like to fill my blender too full when doing this, because if the lid is not securely closed, a big mess might occur.

In a blender container, combine the coconut milk, rice, nuts, dates, kale (if using), maple syrup, vanilla, and cinnamon. Now fill your blender with hot water so it is three-quarters full, about 6 cups of water. Let the ingredients sit in the blender container for 30 minutes. (Alternatively, you can use cold water and let the horchata sit overnight.)

Turn on the blender and whirl, whirl, and twirl. Run the blender for about 3 minutes or until the contents are completely ground up and the liquid is smooth.

Strain the mixture through a cheesecloth or a fine-mesh strainer into a large pitcher. (You definitely want to strain this well or it will be very gritty.) Add 6 cups of cold water to make about 1 gallon, and chill the horchata before drinking (or else pour it over ice).

AFTER-DINNER SNACKS

From a very young age, my eating schedule has been shaped by restaurant schedules. Back in Sweden, when I came home from school my mother was at work, and in the morning when I left for school she was asleep. I often ate dinner with my grandmother, but I loved to stay up late to wait for my mother to return from work. My earliest home "chef" experiences and favorite food memories are preparing an after-dinner snack for my mother. White toast with butter, lots of *löjrom* (Nordic caviar) with white onions, and Arctic shrimp sandwiches were favorite classic Swedish late-night snacks.

For most chefs, cooks, and waitstaff, eating a peaceful dinner in the restaurant where you work isn't actually doable, as there is never peace. It is essential to eat a snack at home to decompress and to feed the soul away from the restaurant. Although you can eat these snacks any time of the day, as a cook or a chef, when you really eat is after the regular dinner has been served. These snacks can be prepared in advance, and many can be frozen and reheated in a flash.

THE 'BU BLACK BEAN NACHOS

SERVES 4

4 cups blue (or any color) tortilla chips, purchased or homemade

2 cups cooked black beans, purchased or homemade, drained

Cheesy Cheese Sauce (recipe follows), warm

2 cups shredded three-cheese blend (Monterey Jack, Colby, and Cheddar cheeses)

1 cup Charred Salsa Roja (page 271)

½ cup sour cream or crème fraîche

2 tablespoons chopped green onions (scallions)

4 cups chopped fresh kale (optional)

TIPS Try sweet corn nachos: Swap the black beans for corn, swap blue tortilla chips for white, and it is the summer spin.

Add cooked ground turkey or beef, and it's chili nachos, so you can chill and eat nachos.

Leftover scallions? Grill them and drizzle with any salsa or vinaigrette in this book.

I'm a chipaholic. I may need an intervention, because sometimes I think that life satisfaction might be directly tied to how much salsa you get to eat. Cheesy, spicy nachos are always a great way to end a stressful night. I usually top my nachos with a mountain of kale or arugula with lemon dressing, which makes them healthy, right?

Preheat the oven to 400°F.

In a skillet or other ovenproof serving dish, layer the chips with the black beans and cheese sauce. Finish with a layer of the shredded three-cheese blend. Bake in the preheated oven, or place under the broiler for a few minutes, until the cheese is melted and brown and crispy on the top.

Remove the nachos from the oven and garnish with the salsa roja, sour cream, green onions, and kale, if using. Ready, set, serve—you deserve this cheesy, gooey mess.

(RECIPE CONTINUES)

CHEESY CHEESE SAUCE

MAKES 1½ CUPS

2 tablespoons salted butter
⅓ cup diced onion
⅓ cup diced green bell pepper
⅓ cup diced red bell pepper
1 jalapeño or serrano chile pepper, diced
1 cup whole milk
1 tablespoon cornstarch
1 cup shredded jalapeño Jack cheese
1 teaspoon salt, or to taste

Heat the butter in a small skillet over medium heat until melted. Add the onion, bell peppers, jalapeño, and 1 tablespoon of water. Sauté the vegetables for about 5 minutes or until they are translucent and soft. We do not want to brown them.

Add the whole milk and bring to a gentle simmer. Meanwhile, combine the cornstarch with 2 tablespoons of water in a small bowl and whisk until no clumps appear. Whisk the cornstarch mixture into the skillet, and continue to stir until the sauce begins to thicken.

Remove the skillet from the heat and stir in the jalapeño Jack cheese until you have a smooth sauce. Add salt to taste, and use while still warm.

This sauce can be chilled and stored for several days before using. Save any extra for mac and cheese, baked potatoes, or roasted cauliflower.

CHARRED SALSA ROJA

MAKES 2 CUPS

2 large Roma tomatoes

¼ cup chopped white or yellow onion

½ cup fresh cilantro, chopped

1 tablespoon canned chipotle chiles in adobo sauce (see Note)

2 tablespoons fresh lime juice (about 1 lime)

2 teaspoons salt

NOTE For additional uses of canned chipotle chiles in adobo sauce, see page 227. If you don't want your salsa too spicy, use only 1 tablespoon of the adobo sauce, and none of the chiles.

You can't go wrong with salsa roja. You can make your salsa roja with raw tomatoes or with charred tomatoes. If you are in a hurry, skip the charring.

Char your tomatoes on a grill or under the broiler set on high until most of the skin is black, about 5 minutes. Allow the tomatoes to cool for a few minutes, then peel off the skin and discard it.

Place the peeled tomatoes, onion, cilantro, chipotle chiles, lime juice, and salt in a food processor or blender, and pulse a few times until combined.

CREAMY AND CRISPY GARBANZO BEAN DIP

MAKES 2 CUPS

1½ cups cooked garbanzo beans (chickpeas), purchased or homemade, drained (see Note, opposite)

4 tablespoons olive oil

½ red onion, diced

½ bell pepper (any color), diced

1 garlic clove, sliced thin

4 tablespoons chopped fresh parsley

2 teaspoon salt, or to taste

3 tablespoons lemon dressing (see page 48)

1 jalapeño pepper, sliced thin

1 cup Crispy Garbanzo Beans (recipe follows)

Toasted pita bread, for serving

TIP Give this dip a holiday spin and garnish with pomegranate seeds.

This dip is super versatile. Serve it warm, drizzled with lemon dressing and fresh herbs, and topped with the crispy beans. Or wrap it up with rice and salsa in a tortilla to make a vegetarian burrito. Shake up your garbanzo bean game by using organic black chickpeas from Timeless natural food.

Place the beans in a food processor and blend until fine.

Add 2 tablespoons olive oil to a medium sauté pan and sauté the onion over medium heat for about 1 minute. Then add the bell pepper and garlic and sauté for about 3 more minutes, stirring frequently, until the onion is translucent. Add half of the parsley and season with salt.

Transfer the cooked onions and peppers to the food processor, and blend with the garbanzo beans until smooth. The dip can be made up to this point 3 days in advance.

To serve, heat the remaining 2 tablespoons oil in a skillet and sauté the dip until it is heated through. Transfer the dip to a small serving bowl and drizzle it with the lemon dressing. Garnish with the remaining parsley, the jalapeño slices, and the Crispy Garbanzo Beans. Serve with toasted pita bread.

NOTE Got liquid from your canned garbanzo beans? Go ahead, make some whipped aquafaba. (*Aqua what?!*) Pour the garbanzo bean liquid into the bowl of a standing mixer; you should have about ¾ cup from a standard 15-ounce can. Add 4 tablespoons confectioners' sugar and a small squeeze of lemon juice (1 teaspoon), and whip for 5 to 8 minutes or until it looks like whipped cream. Then add 2 teaspoons olive oil and 1 teaspoon agave syrup and whip for 1 more minute. Now you've got yourself some pretty tasty vegan and nondairy whipped cream to use with berries on pancakes. And that's aquafaba—also known as aquafabulous.

CRISPY GARBANZO BEANS

MAKES 1 CUP

1 tablespoon vegetable oil

1 cup cooked garbanzo beans (chickpeas), purchased or homemade, drained (see Note)

Salt to taste

Paprika to taste

In a small skillet, heat the oil over medium-high heat, and sauté the garbanzo beans until they are browned and crispy. Transfer the garbanzo beans to a plate to cool, and season with salt and paprika.

CAULIFLOWER AND BROCCOLI 'BU FALAFEL

SERVES 4 TO 6

1 cup chopped cauliflower (about ¼ head)

1 cup chopped broccoli (about ¼ head)

1 (15-ounce) can garbanzo beans (chickpeas), homemade or purchased, drained (see Note, page 273)

1 tablespoon chopped shallot

½ cup chopped fresh parsley

½ cup chopped fresh kale or spinach

1 garlic clove, grated

2 tablespoons fresh lemon juice

3 teaspoons salt

1 cup dry bread crumbs, gluten-free if available

Olive oil

Lime Cucumber Yogurt Sauce (page 277; optional)

Pucker Up Tahini Sauce (page 278; optional)

Falafel is a famously delicious traditional Middle Eastern deep-fried ball made from garbanzo or fava beans. We make ours with the inclusion of broccoli, cauliflower, and kale, and it is sautéed, not fried. Soft, not crispy. It is a falafel who lives by the beach and basks in the sun.

These 'Bu Falafels are great as an appetizer. Or wrap them in soft pita bread with some romaine lettuce, cucumbers, and red onion.

Bring a medium pot of water to a boil. Drop in the cauliflower and broccoli and blanch for 1 minute. The vegetables should still be crispy and undercooked. Drain them and lay them out on paper towels to dry.

Once the cauliflower and broccoli are fully dry, put them in a food processor. Add the chickpeas, shallot, parsley, kale or spinach, garlic, lemon juice, and salt. Pulse until just combined, leaving the mixture slightly chunky. Over-processing is always a bigger crime than under-processing.

Transfer the mixture to a medium bowl and stir in ½ cup of the bread crumbs. Form the mixture into 1-inch balls and flatten the top so they look like crab cakes. Coat both sides of the falafels in the remaining ½ cup bread crumbs. The falafels can be made up to this point several days in advance and refrigerated, and can also be frozen to use at a later date.

(RECIPE CONTINUES)

Heat some oil in a medium skillet over high heat, and sauté about 6 of the falafels (do not crowd the skillet) until they are crisp on all sides and heated through, about 5 minutes. Repeat with the remaining falafels.

To serve, top the falafels with the Lime Cucumber Yogurt Sauce or the Pucker Up Tahini Sauce, or both. Don't feel like making a sauce? You don't need a sauce. You can serve these with any leftover salsa in your fridge, or with a salad tossed with lemon dressing.

LIME CUCUMBER YOGURT SAUCE

MAKES 1½ CUPS

1 cup plain whole-milk or vegan yogurt

1 Persian cucumber or ½ hothouse cucumber, diced fine

1 tablespoon chopped red onion, shallot, or green onions (scallions)

Juice from 1 lime

1 garlic clove, grated

½ cup chopped fresh herbs: cilantro, parsley, mint, chives, or your choice

Salt to taste

2 tablespoons olive oil

TIP To make a thicker dip, place your yogurt in a cheesecloth bag set over a bowl and let the excess liquid drain off for a few hours. Grate or dice the cucumber and mix it with salt to taste. Squeeze out the excess liquid from this cucumber-salt mixture, and then combine it with the drained yogurt and the remaining ingredients.

Use your favorite unflavored yogurt for this recipe—you can even use nondairy yogurt for a vegan take. (My favorite vegan yogurt is Forager cashew yogurt.) This sauce is delicious with lots of things: in a baked potato, alongside grilled fish, with lentils or vegetables, on the 'Bu Falafel (page 274), or as a dip with pita chips. Add jalapeño or serrano chile peppers for a spicy kick.

Mix me all together and I am delish.

Serve me with your favorite dish.

PUCKER UP TAHINI SAUCE

MAKES 1 CUP

½ cup tahini (sesame seed paste)

Juice from 1 lemon

¼ cup hot water

1 garlic clove, grated

3 tablespoons olive oil

Salt to taste

1 tablespoon honey, agave, or maple syrup (optional)

TIP Can you make your own tahini? Yes, of course. Just throw your toasted hulled sesame seeds (about 1 cup) into a food processor and grind them fine. Add a little salt and 2 tablespoons olive or vegetable oil to make a paste. If you have toasted sesame seed oil gathering dust in the fridge, add 1 teaspoon; if not, skip it. And, if desired, add 1 tablespoon honey, agave, or maple syrup for a sweeter sauce.

Tahini is a sesame seed paste. It is bitter, it is complex, it is delicious. It might not be love at first bite, but it is oddly addictive once you begin to savor its distinct puckery taste. It is used mostly with garbanzo beans to make hummus, but it can also shine as the star of the show. You'll typically find beige-colored tahini, but be adventurous and try black tahini paste, available online or in specialty stores, for a cool, mysterious-looking black sauce.

Spoon the tahini into a small bowl, and then add the lemon juice. The mixture will seize up and get stiff, so thin it with the ¼ cup hot water to make a smoother sauce. Add the garlic and olive oil, and season to taste with salt. For a sweeter sauce, stir in the honey, agave, or maple syrup.

SWEDISH-STYLE CHICKEN MEATBALLS

SERVES 4 TO 6

1 pound ground chicken

¼ cup panko bread crumbs soaked in 3 tablespoons milk

¼ cup finely diced peeled carrot (1 small carrot)

¼ cup finely diced yellow onion

¼ cup finely diced bell pepper, any color

½ cup ricotta cheese, drained (to make your own, see Note, page 117)

1 teaspoon paprika

2 teaspoons salt, or to taste

2 tablespoons chopped fresh parsley or cilantro

Zest from 1 lemon or 1 lime

Olive or vegetable oil

Old-School Gravy (recipe follows)

Simple Syrup Cranberries (page 283; optional)

Boiled potatoes (optional)

Swedish food does not have many internationally recognized players. The Ikea meatballs may be the most famous dish of them all! No need to go furniture shopping—you can easily make your own meatballs at home. Swedish meatballs can be made with beef, lamb, pork, or some combination that you like. We make ours with chicken because that is right for Malibu.

Swedish meatballs, like many dishes in Sweden, should be much smaller than their American or Italian cousins. Their size is what makes them Swedish. And to eat them like a Viking, you need a classic brown gravy, cranberries, and potatoes. You can make a large batch and freeze what you don't use right away. It's always nice to have some in the freezer for an easy dinner or late-night snack. To round out a Swedish smorgasbord, cheese in any form is recommended, perhaps a fancy goat cheese log (see page 282).

Our first chef at the restaurant, Dane Skophammer, worked on developing the Malibu version of the Swedish meatball. Dane also helped save my house during the Woolsey fires. So thanks, Dane!

In a medium bowl, combine the chicken, panko, carrot, onion, bell pepper, ricotta, paprika, salt, parsley or cilantro, and lemon or lime zest. Mix together until well combined. (You could sauté the carrot, onion, and green bell pepper in a

(RECIPE CONTINUES)

little oil first, but I skip this step.) Using your hands, form the mixture into 3½-ounce mini-meatballs. Resist your American urge to make the meatballs bigger, because bigger isn't always better—special gifts come in small packages. These meatballs should be 1 inch in diameter—no more!

Heat a little oil in a large skillet over high heat. Sauté the meatballs until they are browned on all sides and cooked through, about 10 minutes. (Alternatively, you can drizzle them with a little oil and bake them on a sheet pan in a preheated 400°F oven for 15 minutes.)

Pour the Old-School Gravy over the meatballs, and serve them with Simple Syrup Cranberries and boiled potatoes if desired.

OLD-SCHOOL GRAVY

MAKES 4 CUPS

TIP Preparing sautéed onion and pureeing it into the gravy is a great way to add body, color, and flavor. See the brisket on page 229 for a similar application. But if you don't like onion or are pressed for time, you can skip the step of adding it to the gravy.

5 tablespoons salted butter
3 tablespoons flour
2 cups chicken broth, purchased or homemade
1 cup heavy cream
1 cup chopped white or yellow onion
1 tablespoon olive or vegetable oil
1 tablespoon plus 2 teaspoons Worcestershire sauce
1 tablespoon fresh lemon juice
1 teaspoon salt, or to taste
1 teaspoon chopped fresh chives (optional)
1 teaspoon whole pink peppercorns (optional)

Melt the butter in a medium saucepan over low heat. Whisk in the flour and cook for 1 minute, until the flour is coated in the butter. Stir in 1 cup of the chicken broth and bring to a low boil. Add the second cup of broth, bring to a light boil again, and then add the heavy cream. Simmer slowly while the sauce thickens, about 5 minutes, or until the sauce

(RECIPE CONTINUES)

is medium thick, smooth, and free of lumps. If you have a bunch of big lumps, no need to despair—just run the gravy through a fine-mesh strainer and return it to the pot.

In a small skillet, cook the onion in the oil over medium-high heat, stirring frequently, until the onion is browned and caramelized, about 10 minutes. Stir in the Worcestershire sauce, and cook for another 5 minutes. The onions will add color to our gravy.

Transfer the onions to a blender, add 1 cup of the gravy, and process until smooth. Return the onion-gravy blend to the rest of the gravy in the pot and stir to combine. Season the gravy with the lemon juice and about 1 teaspoon of salt. Stir in the chives and pink peppercorns, if using. This gravy will keep for 5 days in the fridge.

Pour the gravy over the meatballs and dine like a Viking.

FANCY GOAT CHEESE LOG

MAKES 1 GOAT CHEESE LOG

¼ cup thinly sliced fruit, such as persimmons, strawberries, or kiwi, or any vegetable, such as zucchini or carrots

1 teaspoon fresh herbs, such as parsley, thyme, or dill

1 (8-ounce) goat cheese log

NOTE To make homemade goat cheese, see my first book, *Malibu Farm Cookbook*, page 126.

To complete your Swedish smorgasbord of meatballs, cranberries, and potatoes, you need cheese, because all Swedish smorgasbords have cheese. Fancy-up a store-bought goat cheese log by slicing any fruit or vegetable super thin and pressing it into the top. From plain to fabulous in 5 minutes.

Press the fruit or vegetable and herbs into the goat cheese log and serve.

TIP Substitute any berry in this recipe. Soft berries like raspberries, strawberries, or blueberries do not need to steam in the hot syrup, however; simply add them to the cooled syrup. Use simple syrup berries to make cocktails or mocktails, or sweeten plain yogurt with them.

SIMPLE SYRUP CRANBERRIES

MAKES 2 CUPS

I love cranberries on my pancakes, with my meatballs, in my yogurt, in my oatmeal, and in my apple cake. When we first opened the cafe, we put Swedish pancakes with cranberries on the menu, and no kidding, 99.9 percent of the guests told us they did not like cranberries. We switched the menu to say "berries" and still gave them cranberries, and guess what—99.9 percent of the guests said, "Oh, what kind of berries are these? I like them!" So yeah, you like cranberries, you just don't know it yet. But you will soon.

1 cup sugar
2 cups fresh cranberries (do not use frozen)

Although you can put this straight into a pot on the stove, I make a simple DIY double-boiler to gently steam the cranberries in the syrup. No fancy equipment needed: a medium-size pot and a heatproof metal or glass mixing bowl that fits snug on top of it will work.

In the bowl, combine the sugar and cranberries in ¾ cup water, cover the bowl with plastic wrap or a tight fitting lid, and place over the pot filled with a couple inches of water. Bring the water in the pot to a gentle simmer. Uncover the bowl once to stir to dissolve the sugar. Cook for about 15 minutes or until the first cranberry begins to burst, then remove from the heat. The majority of the cranberries should remain whole so that they don't turn into jam. The goal is have loose cranberries in a simple syrup. Chill the cranberries in the syrup. The simple syrup berries will last 5 days in the fridge.

STOPLIGHT TACO TRIO

SERVES 3 TO 4

12 (3½-inch) corn tortillas

Olive or vegetable oil

1 cup shredded jalapeño Jack cheese

1 cup cooked corn kernels

1 cup cooked black beans, drained

RED TACOS

1 pound skirt steak (or any steak), grilled and chopped

½ cup sliced red cabbage

½ cup sliced red bell pepper

½ to 1 cup Charred Salsa Roja (page 271)

GREEN TACOS

1 pound cooked chicken breast, cubed or shredded

1 cup shaved raw Brussels sprouts tossed with lemon dressing (see page 48)

½ cup Tomatillo Avocado Salsa (recipe follows)

YELLOW TACOS

1 cup Cubed Roasted Butternut Squash (page 54)

1 cup cooked spaghetti squash (see page 183)

⅛ cup Sweet and Hot Habanero Sauce (page 60) or Tabasco sauce

I can eat tacos every day, and I am not alone. Chefs spend the workday in restaurant kitchens making delicious but time-consuming delicacies for their customers. At the end of their shift, what do they want to eat? Yeah, not the food they make at work. They just want a taco. That said, at Malibu Farm our mission is always to increase the amount of greens and vegetables we serve and eat. We aspire to change not just the diets of our customers but also the diets of our team members, especially those in the back of the house. Nothing makes me happier than when I find a newly hired dishwasher adding raw Brussels sprouts to his or her tacos or eating vegetarian yellow tacos. And guess what? It actually happens all the time.

These are called "stoplight" tacos because they are red, green, and yellow. Choose your favorite, make the one you like, mix it up, and combine your favorite ingredients. These are only suggestions from the rainbow of colors in the garden. All ingredients can be prepared ahead. Only cook the chicken and the steak fresh.

Preheat the oven to 375°F.

Place the red/green/yellow toppings in small bowls for a build-your-own taco party. (We use about 2 tablespoons of each ingredient per taco.)

(RECIPE CONTINUES)

NOTE Make your own tortillas? If you're trapped at home in a pandemic or snowstorm, or feeling the blues from the news, absolutely. Following the package instructions, combine masa harina with warm water (usually 2 cups with 1½ cups warm water). Knead together until a dough forms. Divide the dough into 2-tablespoon-size balls and place them between sheets of parchment paper. Using a rolling pin, press down on each ball to create a thin 5-inch round. (Got a tortilla press? Awesome, use it instead; either way will work.) Then sear the tortillas in a large skillet over high heat, flipping them over at least twice, for a 2-minute-total cook time. Eat and repeat. To color up your tortillas, add a drop of beet juice or a few saffron threads to the warm water.

Place the tortillas on a sheet pan, drizzle them with a little oil, and top each tortilla with a heaping tablespoon each of the cheese, corn, and beans. Heat in the oven for 5 to 8 minutes, until the cheese is just melted.

Set the warm tortillas out for guests to help themselves, creating red, green, and/or yellow tacos, or whatever combos they like.

RED TACOS: steak, red cabbage, red bell peppers, Charred Salsa Roja

GREEN TACOS: chicken, Brussels sprouts, Tomatillo Avocado Salsa

YELLOW TACOS: cooked butternut squash, cooked spaghetti squash, habanero salsa

TOMATILLO AVOCADO SALSA

MAKES 2 CUPS

2 avocados, peeled and pitted
6 tomatillos, husks discarded
½ yellow onion, chopped (about ½ cup)
1 jalapeño or serrano chile pepper (serrano is spicier)
1 garlic clove
½ cup fresh cilantro leaves
Juice from 2 limes
1 teaspoon salt, or to taste

In a blender, combine 1 of the avocados with the tomatillos, onion, jalapeño or serrano chile, garlic, cilantro, lime juice, and salt, and process until smooth. Taste for salt and add more if needed. Transfer the mixture to a bowl.

Dice the remaining avocado into medium chunks and stir them in.

OLIVE OIL CHOCOLATE DIPPING SAUCE

SERVES 4 TO 6

1 (10-ounce) bag of your favorite chocolate chips

½ cup olive oil, or more if needed

You can create the perfect chocolate sauce by whisking warm olive oil into dark chocolate chips. I like to use 60 percent semisweet chocolate and 40 percent bittersweet chocolate, but you can use any combination you like. I find 100 percent semisweet chocolate too sweet, and 100 percent bittersweet too bitter, but it is your dip, so do the dip the way you like.

As for what to dip into the chocolate, it's your choice: strawberries, chunks of banana, marshmallows, your own fingers to lick. Then dip again, into chopped nuts, sprinkles, toasted coconut flakes . . .

The perfect end to any night.

Place the chocolate chips in a heatproof medium bowl.

Pour the olive oil into a small skillet and heat it gently over low heat. Do not let it overheat or begin to burn. It should reach a gentle simmer after 2 minutes. Remove the skillet from the heat and pour the oil over the chocolate chips. Whisk the oil into the chocolate chips until you have a smooth sauce. For a thinner sauce, add a little more oil.

The sauce will stay soft and dippalicious if left at room temperature. Not to worry about leftovers—there will be none.

CARAMEL NUTS POPCORN

SERVES 4

1 cup granulated sugar

2 tablespoons honey or light corn syrup

4 tablespoons (½ stick) salted butter

⅛ teaspoon baking soda

4 cups freshly popped popcorn (1 microwavable bag)

1 cup chopped walnuts or any nut of choice

Salt to taste

TIP Color or spice it up! While the caramel is still sticky and warm, dust the popcorn with a flavoring of choice: colorful sprinkles, cinnamon, cayenne pepper, curry powder, or chopped herbs like rosemary or basil.

For kids and kids at heart. Perfect for movie nights, or just watching the stars, dreaming impossible dreams that may one day change the world. Add cayenne pepper to turn up the heat or cinnamon to spice it up.

Place a large dry pot, free of water or any moisture, over medium heat. Add the sugar and honey. Don't touch the pot or stir it, just let it be. Once the contents of the pot begin to melt around the edges, after about 5 minutes, you can gently shake the pot to evenly distribute the melting sweeteners. Once the sweeteners are melted, stir in the butter and the baking soda, and then *quickly* stir in the popcorn and nuts. (If you stir too slowly, you might burn the sweeteners, the popcorn, or both, which we don't want.) Combine until evenly distributed. Add salt to taste.

Spread the caramel popcorn out on a sheet pan and let it cool slightly before eating.

Pull up a chair and eat it under the moonlight. Your home smells like caramel popcorn magic, so this night is going to end all right.

(VACUUM PACKED)
100% PURE COFFEE

Good night, moon.

Good night, Arnold, sleeping under the stars.

Good night, chickens; good night, goats.

Good night, bees and all the fruit trees.

Good night, cat; good night, dogs.

Good night to the ’Bu and to the world. I love u.

COOKING RULES

Well, there are no real rules of the kitchen. That said, cooking *rules*. That is how we feed ourselves and others, it is as ancient as humanity, it is an art form as well as a craft, it can be a hobby or a job, you can do it alone or with others—so put on an apron and start cooking.

Never use an ingredient you do not *love*. Don't be afraid to substitute for something you do love.

Find a **SALT** mate. Learn to season properly by choosing one salt and using it consistently. Different salts have different salt content. Common table salt has 97 to 99 percent sodium chloride and tastes "very salty," and with the fine texture it is easy to over-salt if you are not used to cooking with it. Kosher salt, on the other hand, tastes "less salty" than both table and sea salt. Different textures also yield different results and will make it harder to master the skill of cooking, so choose one salt and stop swinging.

BLACK PEPPER is overrated—don't sprinkle it on everything.

There is no such thing as too much **LEMON**, and lemon dressing is the most important ingredient of all. Every dish needs an acidic punch—lemon, lime, vinegar, soy—but lemon is the queen who rules supreme. Must be fresh-squeezed for cooking. Bottled is for lemonade only.

You must have **MUSTARD**. Whole-grain is my favorite, and with **MAYONNAISE** you can easily make many different aiolis: lemon, spicy, herb, curry.

GARLIC must be fresh from the bulb. Pre-peeled is garbage, so if you have that, *toss it out.*

OLIVE OIL goes with everything. Think of extra-virgin as "extra-low" smoke point, so reserve that for salads and cold applications, but don't use it for high-heat cooking. Switch to regular olive oil for sautéing and baking, and use avocado oil, or a blend of olive/vegetable oil, for higher heat cooking.

SWEET TREATS Maple syrup, honey, and agave make your pantry complete.

I live for **SPICY**. Serrano, jalapeño, and habanero are music to my palate.

ARUGULA IS LIFE, and yes, it goes in everything and with everything.

I love **BUTTER**, but butter burns very easily, so to sauté with it, add some olive oil to raise the smoke point. I don't bother with unsalted butter because I don't need two different butters in my fridge. A dish sweet or savory will need salt anyway, so salted butter it is.

In addition to the preceding, **MY FAVORITE INGREDIENTS** are black beans, garbanzo beans, lentils, farro, quinoa, rice, pasta, butternut squash, beets, potatoes, tomatoes, broccoli, cauliflower, green beans, asparagus, and all other vegetables—*all shapes, all sizes, all colors.*

GARDENING RULES: Grow what grows without a fight and you shall garden without blight. Guess why I love arugula? Yeah, because snails, squirrels, peacocks, coyotes, bunnies, goats, and chickens don't! Just so you know, it is the easiest crop to grow.

ORGANIC RULES: The fight for organics is an environmental issue, not a personal issue. We fight for clean air, clean soil, and clean water. VOTE for the future because your life depends upon it. EAT for the future by consuming fewer animal products. LIVE for the future by creating and consuming less waste. LOVE for the future, including the future of those who appear different, speak other languages, or are from other cultures.

GRATITUDE + APPRECIATION + ACKNOWLEDGMENTS + RECOGNITION

Eight years, nine restaurants. One "cooler lady."

Some things have changed, yet much remains the same. I still live in Malibu, in the same house where it all began. I know that age is just a number, and that there is no time that is too late for you or anyone to be great, or do something great, or just have a great time or a great meal. I believe that even if you don't know, you can learn anything you want to know. I've learned a lot in these past few years about farming, animals, raising kids, building restaurants, and collaborating with team members, but there is still so much to learn. Another day, another problem—but also possible solutions, resolutions, and growth. I've learned that sometimes when we least expect change, it comes for us anyway. The Woolsey fire in November 2018, the spring rainstorms in 2019, and the spread of the coronavirus in early 2020 were brutal reminders of how life can change quickly and unexpectedly. Every year has brought successes and surprises, fears and failures. I don't know where I or my restaurants will be tomorrow—during the height of the pandemic all the restaurants closed down, but they will hopefully reopen—but today it is all about appreciating the journey and expressing gratitude to those who made it possible.

So many people to thank—so many friends and strangers. If I close my eyes and go all the way back to the beginning, my very first mentor was the creator of MAX Burger in Sweden. **CURT BERGFORS**, the owner of the first real restaurant that I worked at, encouraged me to emigrate to the United States. This Swedish restaurateur inspired my American journey.

The Mayor, a.k.a. **MEIR TEPER**, one of my first customers, opened doors I didn't know existed, opportunities I never could have dreamed of. How is it that the owner of Nobu strolls down a deserted pier to a funky pop-up cafe, orders breakfast, and becomes my mentor? I don't know, but suddenly my world got really big, really fast. Thank you! And thanks to **LARRY ELLISON**, **RICK CARUSO**, **DAVID WEINREB**, **NOBU MATSUHISA**, the **WATANABE FAMILY**, the **CHAPUR FAMILY**, and the **HOWARD HUGHES CORPORATION**, license operators.

In my heart I will always be a small-town girl, and I am not sure I could have been brave enough to leave the backyard if not for the encouragement from my husband, **JOHN STOCKWELL**, a contrarian, a Stockopedia, a rule breaker, a fact challenger, a believer in the big, the bold, the crazy, the unconventional, teaching me that the impossible is only so for those who do not believe or those too afraid. YES, JOHN, it was your idea I reach out to the Malibu Pier to host a dinner.

My first Malibu Pier kitchen hire, **EYMARD**. I now know how hard, almost impossible, it is for a woman without a traditional chef background to find a supportive man in the restaurant world, as most men I meet want to school me, tell me, teach me, change me. I quickly gave him the nickname "Eymore," as we always needed more—more people, more product, more space, more cooks, more restaurants—and he was *more* than anyone I could ever wish for. Thank you!

THE TEAM. Some of you are here now and some of you were here then, but you will always be a part of the team who rules: Gerardo, Filemon, Luis, Wilson, Miguel, Geremias, Esteban, Reynaldo, Clemente, Santiago, Ernest, Dane, Thomas, Yanelquis, David, Joey, Matt, Mitch, Pancho, Justin, Tony, Suzy, Cassie, Natalya, Francisco, Amy, Breck, Jaime, Brenda, Rolando, Inez, Fidel, Eddie, Sam, Richie, Anibal, Jonathan, Alex, Patrick, Yahaira, Zan, Lorena. (Forgive me if I've left off anyone's name.)

DONNA LOFFREDO, executive editor, who ended up taking over the project mid-pandemic when our original editor departed. **ERIN KUNKEL**, amazing photographer. **KATHY KAISER**, for her assistance. **MIA JOHNSON**, for her beautiful book design. **MARK McCAUSLIN** and **KELLI TOKOS** for shepherding the book through production. And **KATHERINE COWLES** at the Cowles Agency.

VANESSA ALEXANDER for the interior design that made everyone feel at home.

The cities of **LULEA** and **MALIBU**. I went from one small town to another. You are my home. You are my heart.

MY MOTHER: your wish was my command.

THE TRIPLE C: **CELIA**, **CASPER**, and **CADEN**. You have all taught me more than I have taught you—other than being on time. I am pretty sure I taught you to be punctual.

INDEX

A

Acai Breakfast Bowl, 28
Aioli
- Artichoke, 218
- I Heart You Happiness, 219

Apple(s)
- Cranberry Cake, 167
- The Good Stuffing, 236
- Kale Serrano Hot Sauce, 61
- Salad, The Big, with Brussels Sprouts, 179–80

Aquafaba whipped cream, preparing, 273
Aquavit, Rhubarb-Infused, 262
Artichoke(s)
- Raw, Salad with Fennel, Arugula, and Parmesan, 194–95
- Twice as Nice, and Artichoke Aioli, 216–18

Arugula, 295
- Chicken Parm from the Farm, 115–16
- Fennel, and Parmesan, Raw Artichoke Salad with, 194–95
- Green Chimichurri, 108
- The Open-Face Salad Omelet, 46–48

Asparagus
- Easy-Peasy Veggie Chicken Stir-Fry, 222–23
- Salad, Dillovely, 199–200

Avocado(s)
- ABC Breakfast Tacos, 45
- Pizza, 247–48
- Tomatillo Salsa, 286
- Tomatillo Salsa Verde, 50
- Vegan Chop Salad, 77–79

B

Bacon
- ABC Breakfast Tacos, 45
- Adobo Butter, Smoky, Spicy, 227
- Balsamic Onion Jam, 82
- -Cheese-Corn Panini, 89–90
- Lemon Saffron Pasta Farm-onara, 85

Banana
- Chocolate Vegan Pancakes, 39–40
- Kale-fornia Smoothie, 158
- Strawberry-Tops Shake, 156

Basil Sour Cream Frosting, Green, 163
Bean(s)
- Black, Nachos, The 'Bu, 269–71
- Cauliflower and Broccoli 'Bu Falafel, 274–78
- Chicken Nacho Tortilla Salad, 71–72
- Easy-Peasy Veggie Chicken Stir-Fry, 222–23
- Garbanzo, Crispy, 273
- Garbanzo, Dip, Creamy and Crispy, 272–73
- Green Eggs and Ham, 49–50
- Grilled Salmon Kale Niçoise Salad, 73–74
- Holiday, Red and Green, 241–43
- Stoplight Taco Trio, 284–86
- Surfers Rancheros, 53–54
- Vegan Chop Salad, 77–79

Beef
- Burger, The 'Bu, with Bacon Balsamic Onion Jam, 81–82
- Grandma's Brisket with Onion Gravy, 229–32
- The Real Big Steak with Smoky, Spicy Bacon Adobo Butter, 224–28
- Stoplight Taco Trio, 284–86

Beet(s)
- hummus, preparing, 79
- It, Just Beet It, 94
- Marinated Roasted, Classic, 79
- Pretty in Pink Cheesecake, 159–63
- Pytt i Panna, 55–56
- Raw, Dressing, 94
- Vegan Chop Salad, 77–79
- Yellow, Dressing, 97

Berry(ies). *See also specific berries*
- Acai Breakfast Bowl, 28
- Coconut French Toast, 32
- Meringue, Very, 143–44

Beverages
- Coconut Horchata, 266
- Fresh Mint Tea, 155
- Frozen Rosé Cocktail, 261
- Kale-fornia Smoothie, 158
- Mimosa Rainbow Flight, 265
- Rhubarb-Infused Aquavit, 262
- Strawberry-Tops Shake, 156

Black pepper, 294
Bread. *See also* Tortilla(s)
- Coconut Berry French Toast, 32
- The Good Stuffing, 236
- Pudding, Pumpkin Chocolate, 151–52
- Zucchini, 168

Broccoli and Cauliflower 'Bu Falafel, 274–78
Brussels Sprouts
- The Big Apple Salad with, 179–80
- Monster Sprouts with Hot Honey Dip, 189–90
- Stoplight Taco Trio, 284–86

Burger, The 'Bu Beef, with Bacon Balsamic Onion Jam, 81–82
Butter, 295
- Blue Cheese, 227–28
- Great Ginger, 228
- Lemon Capers, 228
- Smoky, Spicy Bacon Adobo, 227

C

Cabbage
  Vegan 'Bu Thai Noodles, 207–8
  The Whole Fillet Fish Taco, 201–2
Caffe Latte Ice Cream, 140
Cakes
  Apple Cranberry, 167
  Granola Coconut Carrot, 148–50
  Pretty in Pink Cheesecake, 159–63
Candied Nuts and Seeds, 128–31
Capers Lemon Butter, 228
Caramel Nuts Popcorn, 290
Carrot(s)
  Cake, Granola Coconut, 148–50
  Colossal, with Carrot Lime Dressing, 98–99
  Lime Dressing, 99
  Soup with Roasted Tomato Coulis, 177–78
  Vegan 'Bu Thai Noodles, 207–8
Carrot Top Pesto, 116
Cauliflower
  The Big Steak, with Red or Green Chimichurri, 107–9
  and Broccoli 'Bu Falafel, 274–78
  "Potatoes," Faux Parmesan, 118
  Vegetable-Crust Pizzas, 67–69
Cheese
  ABC Breakfast Tacos, 45
  Avocado Pizza, 247–48
  Blue, Butter, 227
  The 'Bu Black Bean Nachos, 269–71
  Chicken Parm from the Farm, 115–16
  -Corn-Bacon Panini, 89–90
  Fancy Goat Cheese Log, 282
  Faux Parmesan Cauliflower "Potatoes," 118
  Greek Salad Pizza, 253
  homemade ricotta, preparing, 117
  Lime-Cilantro Dressing, 196
  Parmesan Lemon Dressing, 200
  Pretty in Pink Cheesecake, 159–63
  Ricotta Cream, 248
  Sauce, Cheesy, 270
  Spaghetti Squash Lasagna, 183–85
  Stoplight Taco Trio, 284–86
  vegan ricotta, preparing, 184
  Vegetable-Crust Pizzas, 67–69
  The Whole Fillet Fish Taco, 201–2
Cherry Cashew Coconut Ice Cream, Vegan, 137
Chicken
  with Grainy Mustard-Rosemary Sauce, 223
  Meatballs, Swedish-Style, 279–83
  Nacho Tortilla Salad, 71–72
  Parm from the Farm, 115–16
  Stoplight Taco Trio, 284–86
  Veggie Stir-Fry, Easy-Peasy, 222–23
Chile Peppers, 295
  Green Jalapeño Harissa, 50
  Grilled Salmon with Miso Tahini Sauce, 205–6
  Kale Apple Serrano Hot Sauce, 61
  Pickled Fresno, Real or Fake?, 113
  Ricotta Cream, 248
  Roasted Poblano Sauce, 246
  Sweet and Hot Habanero Sauce, 60
Chimichurri
  Green, 108
  Red, 109
Chocolate
  Banana Vegan Pancakes, 39–40
  Olive Oil Dipping Sauce, 289
  Pumpkin Bread Pudding, 151–52
Cilantro
  Charred Salsa Roja, 271
  Crema, 202
  Cucumber Lime Gazpacho, 117
  Green Jalapeño Harissa, 50
  -Lime Dressing, 196
Citrus Dressing, Seriously, 48
Coconut
  Berry French Toast, 32
  Crispy Oats, 42
  flour, making your own, 266
  Frosting, 150
  Horchata, 266
  milk, making your own, 266
Corn
  -Cheese-Bacon Panini, 89–90
  The Good Stuffing, 236
  Stoplight Taco Trio, 284–86
  Sweet, Ice Cream, 139
  Sweet, Polenta, 214
  Wedge Salad, The Street, 196
Cranberry
  Apple Cake, 167
  Simple Syrup, 283
Crème Brûlée, Saffron Lemon, 145–47
Crème fraîche
  Cilantro Crema, 202
  cooking with, 118
  Faux Parmesan Cauliflower "Potatoes," 118
  Horseradish Cream, 56
Cucumber(s)
  Greek Salad Pizza, 253
  Lime Gazpacho, 117
  Lime Yogurt Sauce, 277

D

Date Me Dessert, 164
Dillovely Asparagus Salad, 199–200
Dips
  Garbanzo Bean, Creamy and Crispy, 272–73
  Hot Honey, 190
Dressings
  Black Olive Vinaigrette, 112
  Carrot Lime, 99
  Classic Chop, 78
  Green Salsa, 72
  Lime-Cilantro, 196
  making horseradish vinaigrette, 56
  Mustard Lemon, 195
  Mustard Maple, 180
  Niçoise Olive, 74
  Parmesan Lemon, 200
  Raw Beet, 94
  Red Salsa, 72

Dressings (*cont.*)
Seriously Citrus, 48
Soy Lime, 208
Yellow Beet, 97
Yuzu, 125

E

Eggplant
Orange You Glad, 186–88
Ratatouille Boats, 121–22
Eggs
ABC Breakfast Tacos, 45
Green, and Ham, 49–50
Grilled Salmon Kale Niçoise Salad, 73–74
Lemon Saffron Pasta Farm-onara, 85
Lobster Louisa Rolls, 126
The Open-Face Salad Omelet, 46–48
Pytt i Panna, 55–56
Surfers Rancheros, 53–54

F

Falafel, Cauliflower and Broccoli 'Bu, 274–78
Farro and Quinoa, White Rice with, 210
Fish
Charred Octopus with Poblano Salsa, 244–46
Grilled, with Greek Salad and Crudités, 213
Grilled Salmon Kale Niçoise Salad, 73–74
Grilled Salmon with Miso Tahini Sauce, 205–6
Mahimahi with Black Olive Vinaigrette, 111–12
Poke'viche, 93
Pytt i Panna, 55–56
Taco, The Whole Fillet, 201–2
French Toast, Coconut Berry, 32
Frosting
Coconut, 150
Green Basil Sour Cream, 163
Fruit. *See also specific fruits*
Earth Mother Yogurt Bowl, 31
Fancy Goat Cheese Log, 282
Very Berry Meringue, 143–44

G

Gardening tips, 295
Garlic, 295
Gazpacho, Cucumber Lime, 117
Ginger Butter, Great, 228
Grains. *See also specific grains*
Holiday Healthy, 239–40
Granola
Coconut Carrot Cake, 148–50
Earth Mother Yogurt Bowl, 31
Gravy, Old-School, 281–82
Greens. *See also specific greens*
Chicken Nacho Tortilla Salad, 71–72
Dillovely Asparagus Salad, 199–200

H

Harissa, Green Jalapeño, 50
Herbs. *See specific herbs*
Honey Dip, Hot, 190
Horchata, Coconut, 266
Horseradish
Cream, 56
homemade prepared, note on, 56
vinaigrette, preparing, 56
Hummus
beet, preparing, 79
Greek Salad Pizza, 253

I

Ice Cream
Caffe Latte, 140
Sweet Corn, 139
Vegan Cashew Coconut Cherry, 137
Ingredient notes, 294–95

J

Jam, Bacon Balsamic Onion, 82

K

Kale
Apple Serrano Hot Sauce, 61
The Big Apple Salad with Brussels Sprouts, 179–80
-fornia Smoothie, 158
Grilled, Thrills, 193
Grilled Salmon Niçoise Salad, 73–74
Vegan Chop Salad, 77–79

L

Lasagna, Spaghetti Squash, 183–85
Lemon(s), 294
Capers Butter, 228
Mustard Dressing, 195
Parmesan Dressing, 200
Saffron Crème Brûlée, 145–47
Saffron Pasta Farm-onara, 85
Seriously Citrus Dressing, 48
Lentils
Red, Delicata Squash with, 104
Red and Green Holiday Beans, 241–43
Lettuce
Chopped Lobster Salad, 123–25
The Street Corn Wedge Salad, 196
Vegan Chop Salad, 77–79
Lime(s)
Carrot Dressing, 99
-Cilantro Dressing, 196
Cucumber Gazpacho, 117
Cucumber Yogurt Sauce, 277
Seriously Citrus Dressing, 48
Soy Dressing, 208
Lobster
Louisa Rolls, 126
Salad, Chopped, 123–25

M

Mahimahi with Black Olive Vinaigrette, 111–12
Malibu Farms, 12–20
Maple Mustard Dressing, 180
Mayonnaise
Homemade, 218–219
making aioli with, 294
Meatballs, Swedish-Style Chicken, 279–83
Meringue, Very Berry, 143–44
Mimosa Rainbow Flight, 265
Mint, Fresh, Tea, 155
Miso Tahini Sauce, 206
Mustard, 294
Lemon Dressing, 195
Maple Dressing, 180

N

Nachos, The 'Bu Black Bean, 269–71
Noodles, Vegan 'Bu Thai, 207–8
Nuts. *See also specific nuts*
Caramel, Popcorn, 290
and Seeds, Candied, 128–31

O

Oats
Coconut Crispy, 42
Crispy, + Pumpkin Pancakes, 36
Octopus, Charred, with Poblano Salsa, 244–46
Olive Oil, 295
Olive Oil Chocolate Dipping Sauce, 289
Olive(s)
Black, Vinaigrette, 112
Niçoise, Dressing, 74
Omelet, The Open-Face Salad, 46–48
Onion(s)
Bacon Balsamic Jam, 82
Gravy, Grandma's Brisket with, 229–32
Quick Faux Pickled Red, 211
Oranges
Chopped Lobster Salad, 123–25
Seriously Citrus Dressing, 48
Organic foods, 295

P

Pancakes
Pumpkin, + Crispy Oats, 36
Vegan Chocolate Banana, 39–40
Parsley
Green Chimichurri, 108
Green Jalapeño Harissa, 50
Roasted Poblano Sauce, 246
Pasta
Lemon Saffron Farm-onara, 85
Rainbow Pearl Couscous with Romanesco, 103
Ratatouille Boats, 121–22
Pearl Couscous, Rainbow, with Romanesco, 103
Pecans or Walnuts, Crispy, 131
Peppers. *See also* Chile peppers
Ratatouille Boats, 121–22
Red Bell, Roasted and Marinated, 243
Red Chimichurri, 109
Sweet and Hot Habanero Sauce, 60
Pesto, Carrot Top, 116
Pickled Fresno Chile Peppers Real or Fake?, 113
Pico de Gallo, 202
Pizza Dough, Miami Homemade, 254–55
Pizzas
Avocado, 247–48
Greek Salad, 253
Vegetable Crust, 67–69
Poke'viche, 93
Polenta, Sweet Corn, 214
Popcorn, Caramel Nuts, 290
Pork. *See also* Bacon
Green Eggs and Ham, 49–50
Potato(es)
Grilled Salmon Kale Niçoise Salad, 73–74
Pytt i Panna, 55–56
Salad, Beach Picnic, 86–88
Surfers Rancheros, 53–54
Sweet, Fries, Baked, 235
Pudding
Bread, Pumpkin Chocolate, 151–52
Date Me Dessert, 164
Pumpkin(s)
Chocolate Bread Pudding, 151–52
Mini, Jack Be Little, 240
Pancakes + Crispy Oats, 36
saving seeds from, 128
Pytt i Panna, 55–56

Q

Quinoa
and Farro, White Rice with, 210
Holiday Healthy Grains, 239–40
Pumpkin Pancakes + Crispy Oats, 36
Vegan Chocolate Banana Pancakes, 39–40

R

Ratatouille Boats, 121–22
Rhubarb-Infused Aquavit, 262
Rice
Coconut Horchata, 266
Holiday Healthy Grains, 239–40
White, with Farro and Quinoa, 210
Romanesco, Rainbow Pearl Couscous with, 103

S

Saffron
Lemon Crème Brûlée, 145–47
Lemon Pasta Farm-onara, 85
Salads
Beach Picnic Potato, 86–88
Beet It, Just Beet It, 94
The Big Apple, with Brussels Sprouts, 179–80
Chicken Nacho Tortilla, 71–72
Chopped Lobster, 123–25
Colossal Carrots with Carrot Lime Dressing, 98–99

Salads (*cont.*)
Dillovely Asparagus, 199–200
Greek, and Crudités, Grilled Fish with, 213
Greek, Pizza, 253
Grilled Salmon Kale Niçoise, 73–74
Raw Artichoke, with Fennel, Arugula, and Parmesan, 194–95
The Street Corn Wedge, 196
Tomato, Summer, 97
Vegan Chop, 77–79
Salmon
Grilled, Kale Niçoise Salad, 73–74
Grilled, with Miso Tahini Sauce, 205–6
Pytt i Panna, 55–56
Salsa
Dressing, Green, 72
Dressing, Red, 72
Pico de Gallo, 202
Roja, Charred, 271
Tomatillo, Verde, 50
Tomatillo Avocado, 286
Salt, 294
Sandwiches
Cheese-Corn-Bacon Panini, 89–90
Lobster Louisa Rolls, 126
Sauces. *See also* Salsa
Artichoke Aioli, 218
Cheesy Cheese, 270
Cilantro Crema, 202
Classic Creamy Béchamel, 185
Green Chimichurri, 108
Habanero, Sweet and Hot, 60
Homemade Mayonnaise, 218–19
Horseradish Cream, 56
Hot, Kale Apple Serrano, 61
I Heart You Happiness Aioli, 219
Lime Cucumber Yogurt, 277
Miso Tahini, 206
Olive Oil Chocolate Dipping, 289
Pucker Up Tahini, 278
Red Chimichurri, 109
Roasted Poblano, 246
Secret Stir-Fry, 223
Tequila, 152
Scallops
choosing, 123
Chopped Lobster Salad, 123–25
Seeds and Nuts, Candied, 128–31
Sesame seeds, making tahini with, 278
Shake, Strawberry-Tops, 156
Shellfish
Chopped Lobster Salad, 123–25
Lobster Louisa Rolls, 126
Smoothie, Kale-fornia, 158
Sorbet, Strawberry-Tops, 138
Soups
Carrot, with Roasted Tomato Coulis, 177–78
Cucumber Lime Gazpacho, 117
Sour Cream
Basil Frosting, Green, 163
Tofu, 109
Soy Lime Dressing, 208
Spinach
Classic Creamy Béchamel, 185
Green Eggs and Ham, 49–50
Vegan Veggie Scramble with Tofu, 59
Squash. *See also* Pumpkin(s); Zucchini
Butternut, Cubed Roasted, 54
Delicata, with Red Lentils, 104
Holiday Healthy Grains, 239–40
Pytt i Panna, 55–56
saving seeds from, 128
Spaghetti, Lasagna, 183–85
Stoplight Taco Trio, 284–86
Surfers Rancheros, 53–54
Vegan Chop Salad, 77–79
Vegan Veggie Scramble with Tofu, 59
Stir-Fry Sauce, Secret, 221
Strawberries
Frozen Rosé Cocktail, 261
Strawberry-Tops Shake, 156
Strawberry-Tops Sorbet, 138
Stuffing, The Good, 236
Sweeteners, 295
Sweet Potato Fries, Baked, 235

T

Taco(s)
Breakfast, ABC, 45
Fish, The Whole Fillet, 201–2
Trio, Stoplight, 284–86
Tahini
making your own, 278
Miso Sauce, 206
Sauce, Pucker Up, 278
Tea, Fresh Mint, 155
Tequila Sauce, 152
Tofu
making vegan ricotta with, 184
Sour Cream, 109
Vegan 'Bu Thai Noodles, 207–8
Vegan Veggie Scramble with, 59
Tomatillo
Avocado Salsa, 286
Salsa Verde, 50
Tomato(es)
Charred Salsa Roja, 271
Grilled Fish with Greek Salad and Crudités, 213
The Open-Face Salad Omelet, 46–48
Pico de Gallo, 202
Ratatouille Boats, 121–22
Red Chimichurri, 109
Roasted, Coulis, 178
Salad, Summer, 97
Vegan Chop Salad, 77–79
Vegan Veggie Scramble, 59
Vegetable-Crust Pizzas, 67–69
Tortilla(s)
ABC Breakfast Tacos, 45
The 'Bu Black Bean Nachos, 269–71
making your own, 286
Salad, Chicken Nacho, 71–72
Stoplight Taco Trio, 284–86
Surfers Rancheros, 53–54
The Whole Fillet Fish Taco, 201–2

V

Vegetable(s). *See also specific vegetables*
Crust Pizzas, 67–69
Easy-Peasy Veggie Chicken Stir-Fry, 222–23
Fancy Goat Cheese Log, 282
Grilled Fish with Greek Salad and Crudités, 213
Vodka
Frozen Rosé Cocktail, 261
Rhubarb-Infused Aquavit, 262

W

Waffles, I Heart You Gluten-Free, 35
Walnuts
Apple Cranberry Cake, 167
Caramel Nuts Popcorn, 290
or Pecans, Crispy, 131
Zucchini Bread, 168
Wine
Frozen Rosé Cocktail, 261
Mimosa Rainbow Flight, 265

Y

Yogurt
Bowl, Earth Mother, 31
Sauce, Lime Cucumber, 277
Strawberry-Tops Shake, 156
Yuzu Dressing, 125

Z

Zucchini
Bread, 168
pizza crust, preparing, 68
Pytt i Panna, 55–56
Ratatouille Boats, 121–22
Vegan 'Bu Thai Noodles, 207–8

ABOUT THE AUTHOR

Helene Henderson learned to cook in Sweden, where she grew up. In 1997, she started Lavender Farms Catering in Los Angeles, specializing in organic food. Malibu Farm began in her backyard with cooking classes and catered farm dinners. Now she is the chef-owner of Malibu Farm, and the restaurant has expanded to eight cities. She lives in Malibu with her husband, screenwriter and director John Stockwell, and their three children.

For more information, Helene and the farm can be reached at cookingquestions@malibu-farm.com

Published in the United States by Clarkson Potter/Publishers, an imprint of Random House, a division of Penguin Random House LLC, New York. clarksonpotter.com

CLARKSON POTTER is a trademark and POTTER with colophon is a registered trademark of Penguin Random House LLC.

Photographer: Erin Kunkel
Designer: Mia Johnson
Editor: Donna Loffredo
Assistant editor: Katherine Leak
Production editor: Mark McCauslin
Copyeditor: Kathie Ness
Production manager: Kelli Tokos
Compositors: Merri Ann Morrell, Hannah Hunt
Indexer: Elizabeth T. Parson

10 9 8 7 6 5 4 3 2 1

First Edition

Library of Congress Cataloging-in-Publication Data
Names: Henderson, Helene, author.
Title: Malibu Farm: sunrise to sunset / Helene Henderson.
Description: First edition. | New York : Clarkson Potter [2021] | Includes index.
Identifiers: LCCN 2020045358 (print) | LCCN 2020045359 (ebook) | ISBN 9780593138724 | ISBN 9780593138731 (ebook)
Subjects: LCSH: Cooking, American—California style.
| LCGFT: Cookbooks.
Classification: LCC TX715.2.C34 H45 2021 (print) | LCC TX715.2.C34 (ebook) | DDC 641.59794—dc23
LC record available at https://lccn.loc.gov/2020045358.
LC ebook record available at https://lccn.loc.gov/2020045359.

ISBN 978-0-593-13872-4
Ebook ISBN 978-0-593-13873-1

Printed in China